ESPN

PERSONAL LIFE

△

WORK

²× F

$$P^2 = \heartsuit + V + \$$$

$$\$ = 10002 + \square$$

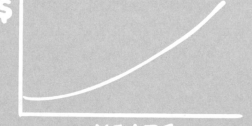

$

YEARS

F

ACTUAL ↓ < REAL ↓

ACTUAL ↑ < REAL ↑

THE

Algebra

OF

Happiness

THE
Algebra
OF
Happiness

Notes on the Pursuit of
Success, Love, and Meaning

SCOTT GALLOWAY

PORTFOLIO / PENGUIN

Portfolio / Penguin
An imprint of Penguin Random House LLC
penguinrandomhouse.com

Copyright © 2019 by Scott Galloway
Illustrations by Kyle Scallon, except p. 162
by Julia Cagninelli and pp. 94, 133, 151 by Zac Norris
Illustration art director: Julia Cagninelli

Most Portfolio books are available at a discount when purchased in quantity for sales promotions or corporate use. Special editions, which include personalized covers, excerpts, and corporate imprints, can be created when purchased in large quantities. For more information, please call (212) 572-2232 or e-mail specialmarkets @penguinrandomhouse.com. Your local bookstore can also assist with discounted bulk purchases using the Penguin Random House corporate Business-to-Business program. For assistance in locating a participating retailer, e-mail B2B@penguinrandomhouse.com.

Library of Congress Cataloging-in-Publication Data

Names: Galloway, Scott, 1964- author.
Title: The algebra of happiness : notes on the pursuit of success,
love, and meaning / Scott Galloway.
Description: New York : Portfolio, 2019.
Identifiers: LCCN 2019001341 (print) | LCCN 2019004441 (ebook) |
ISBN 9780593084182 (ebook) | ISBN 9780593084199 (hardback)
Subjects: LCSH: Self-actualization (Psychology) | Happiness. | Success. |
BISAC: SELF-HELP / Personal Growth / Happiness. | SELF-HELP /
Personal Growth / Success. | BUSINESS & ECONOMICS / Motivational.
Classification: LCC BF637.S4 (ebook) | LCC BF637.S4 G355 2019 (print) |
DDC 650.1--dc23
LC record available at https://lccn.loc.gov/2019001341

Printed in the United States of America
7th Printing

Book design by Cassandra Garruzzo

For
George Thomas Galloway
(aka Dad)

Contents

THE

Algebra

—— OF ——

Happiness

Introduction

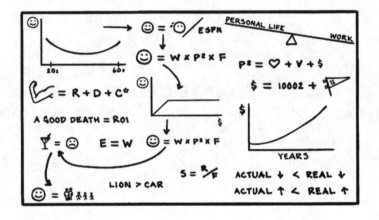

The Algebra of Happiness

IN 2002, I joined the faculty of NYU's Stern School of Business. More than five thousand students have taken my Brand Strategy course.

My students are an impressive group, ranging from Marines from Georgia to IT consultants from Delhi. They are there to learn the time value of money, strategy, and consumer behavior. But our time together frequently veers from brand strategy to life strategies: What career should I choose? How can I set myself up for success? How do I reconcile ambition with personal growth? What can I do now so that I don't have regrets when I'm forty, fifty, or eighty?

We address these questions in the most popular session: the final, three-hour lecture titled "The Algebra of Happiness." In the session, we examine success, love, and the definition of a life well lived. In May 2018, we posted an abridged version on

YouTube. The video was viewed by over 1 million people in the first ten days. My publisher was nudging me to write a follow-up book to *The Four: The Hidden DNA of Amazon, Apple, Facebook, and Google*, and much to her horror, I informed her my second book would be about happiness.

I have no academic credibility or credentials to indicate I should counsel people on how to live their lives. I've had several businesses fail, was divorced by thirty-four, and recently had the most successful venture capitalist in history contact the partners at General Catalyst—my backers at L2—to discourage them (no joke) from investing in L2 because I was "insane." Note: General Catalyst invested anyway and did (really) well.

In fact, you'd need to squint pretty hard to view my life as a framework for happiness. I grew up an unremarkable kid in California in the seventies, skinny and awkward. I got mediocre grades, and didn't test well either. I applied to UCLA and was rejected, which didn't seem like a big deal—my father assured me that "Someone with your street smarts doesn't need college." I had no street smarts, just a father with a new family who didn't want to pay for college. He did, however, secure me a job installing shelving. The job paid $15 to $18 an hour, which seemed like a lot of money. I could buy a nice car, my only real goal at the time.

During twelfth grade, after school, we'd walk into Westwood Village and get ice cream. My friends would shoplift. I'd head home when my friends started shoving Peter Frampton shirts into their pants—not because I was more ethical than them, but because my single mother couldn't handle a call from the LAPD to come get me. Walking back from Westwood Village I crossed Hilgard Avenue, where UCLA sororities lined the street. It was homecoming week, and there were thousands of young women standing in front of their houses singing songs and generally looking like a cross between a Norman Rockwell painting and a late-night Cinemax movie.

At that moment, I decided I needed to go to college and went home to write another letter to UCLA admissions. I told them the truth: "I am a native son of California, raised by an immigrant single mother who is a secretary, and if you don't let me in, I'm going to be installing shelving for the rest of my life." They admitted me nine days before classes started. My mom told me that, as the first person to attend college on either side of the family, I could now "do anything."

As my options were now limitless, I committed to spending the next five years smoking a shit-ton of pot, playing sports, and watching the Planet of the Apes trilogy several dozen times, only taking breaks from this routine for random sexual encounters. Except for the last part, I was hugely successful.

By senior year, most of my friends were getting their act together, focusing on grades, grad school, or getting a job. As no good deed goes unpunished, I rewarded the generosity of California taxpayers and the vision of the Regents of the Unversity of California with a 2.27 GPA. I needed a fifth year at UCLA, as I had failed seven classes and didn't have the credits to graduate. Again, not a big deal, as there were more pot and sci-fi movies to be consumed, and there was nothing compelling waiting for me in the real world.

My last year I had a roommate who was very ambitious, and I felt an odd sense of competition with him. He was obsessed with being an investment banker. I didn't know what investment banking was, but if Gary wanted to do it, I would do it, too. I interviewed well, lied about my grades, and secured a job as an analyst with Morgan Stanley. It helped that the head of the group, like me, had rowed crew in college and had decided that all oarsmen were destined to be great investment bankers.

After an unremarkable stint in investment banking, I decided I'd apply to business school, as I had no idea what I wanted to do, and my girlfriend and best friend were both headed to B-school. The state of California took yet another risk on me, and I was admitted to Berkeley's Haas School of Business. During my second year I was inspired by a professor, David Aaker, who taught brand strategy. While still in school, I founded a strategy firm, Prophet. Prophet did well, and I eventually sold it to Dentsu. In 1997, we decided to incubate several e-commerce firms in the basement of Prophet's office, as that's what an MBA with a shaved head did in the nineties in San Francisco. In sum, I was beginning to hit my stride with the winds of processing power and the internet at my back.

One of the firms, Red Envelope, got swept up in the prosperity of the age, culminating in a NASDAQ IPO—the only retail IPO of 2002. Blessed with extraordinarily good luck, a great partner (my wife), and the wisdom to be born into the most prosperous era in history, I decided that rather than take stock of my blessings, I wanted more. More, goddammit. I wasn't sure what "more" meant . . . so I opted for different. I resigned from the board of Red Envelope, asked my wife for a divorce, moved to New York City, and joined the faculty of NYU's Stern School of Business. (The correct diagnosis of me in my thirties was "character deficiency.")

In 2010, while on the faculty at Stern, I published a piece of research ranking luxury brands based on their digital competence. Many of the firms I had researched reached out, and recognizing there was a commercial opportunity, I founded the business intelligence firm L2. L2 now works with a third of the hundred-largest consumer firms in the world. In 2017, L2 was acquired by Gartner, a publicly traded research firm (NASDAQ: IT).

In entrepreneurship, the highs are very high and the lows very low. I struggle with mild depression (anger, mostly) and spend a lot of time thinking about how to manage it without medication or therapy (note: sometimes one or both are necessary). This struggle has led me to a pursuit of knowledge on how to achieve not only success but happiness. I share my findings on my blog, *No Mercy / No Malice*, but not in any organized fashion. This book is an attempt to remedy that.

In the pages that follow, I'll share what I've observed as a serial entrepreneur, academic, husband, dad, son, and American man, coupled with a decent amount of research. It's important to acknowledge that my thoughts in this book are observations, and not peer-reviewed academic research or a map sketched by someone who has already arrived.

I've shaped this book into four sections. The first outlines the basic equations my students and I review together each spring: if one were to boil down the formula for happiness into a finite number of equations, what would they be? The second part delves deeper into what I've learned about success, ambition, career, and money from my experience as an investment banker, entrepreneur, business school professor, and voice on the impact of big tech on our economy and society.

The topics in sections one and two are meaningful. However, the subject matter in section three is profound: love and relationships. Young people, especially young men, struggle to square the mixed messages about how to thread the needle of relationships and success to achieve personal and professional meaning in our capitalist world. The fourth and last section challenges the reader to turn to the (wo)man in the mirror and address issues including the care and feeding of a physical body, inner demons, and our last days on earth.

Taking life advice from a depressed and insane professor may not make sense. Maybe. But I've done my homework, and for the next two hundred–odd pages, I'm *your* insane professor. I hope these no mercy / no malice observations on success and love help you register a more rewarding life.

The Basics

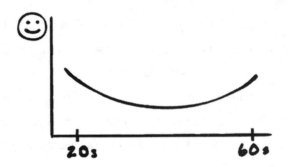

Everyone Knows Happiness, Stress, Tragedy

Your childhood, teens, and college years are the stuff of Han Solo, beer, road trips, random sexual encounters, and self-discovery. Pure magic. From your mid-twenties through your mid-forties, though, shit gets real—work, stress, and the realization that, despite what your teachers and your mom told you, you likely won't be a senator or have a fragrance named after you. As you age, the stress of building the life you've been told you deserve, and are capable of, takes a toll. Also, somebody you love gets sick and dies, and the harshness of life comes into full view.

Then, in your fifties (earlier if you're soulful), you begin to register all the wonderful blessings that are everywhere. I mean everywhere. Beautiful beings that look and smell like you (children). Water that turns into waves you can ride and other wonders of nature. The ability to deliver some sort of sweat or intelligence that people will pay you for, that you can then support your family with. The chance to travel across the surface of the atmosphere at near the speed of sound so you can see amazing things extraordinary people have built. And when tragedy strikes, many times the tragedy is beaten back by our best ideas: science. You recognize that your time here is limited, start smelling the roses, and begin affording yourself the happiness you deserve.

So if in adulthood you find you're stressed, even unhappy at times, recognize that this is a normal part of the journey and just keep on keepin' on. Happiness is waiting for you.

Work It While You're Young

We all know somebody who's successful, in great shape, plays in a band, is close with their parents, volunteers at the ASPCA, and has a food blog. Assume you're not that person. Balance when establishing your career, in my view, is largely a myth. "Struggle porn" will tell you that you must be miserable before you can be successful. This isn't true: you can experience a lot of reward along the way to success. But if balance is your priority in your youth, then you need to accept that, unless you are a genius, you may not reach the upper rungs of economic security.

The slope of the trajectory for your career is (unfairly) set in the first five years post-graduation. If you want the trajectory to be steep, you'll need to burn a lot of fuel. The world is not yours for the taking, but for the trying. Try hard, really hard.

I have a lot of balance now. It's a function of the lack of it in my twenties and thirties. From twenty-two to thirty-four, other than business school, I remember work and not much else. The world does not belong to the big, but to the fast. You want to cover more ground in less time than your peers. This is partially built on talent, but mostly on strategy and endurance. My lack of balance as a young professional cost me my marriage, my hair, and arguably my twenties. There's no user manual here, and it's a trade-off. My lack of balance, while affording me more balance later in life, came at a very real cost.

Sweat

The ratio of time you spend sweating to watching others sweat is a forward-looking indicator of your success. Show me a guy who watches ESPN every night, spends all day Sunday watching football, and doesn't work out, and I'll show you a future of anger and failed relationships. Show me someone who sweats every day and spends as much time playing sports as watching them on TV, and I'll show you someone who is good at life.

The Most Important Decision You Will Make

MOST BUSINESS school students devote their greatest efforts to shaping their work lives and socializing with their friends. However, the most important decision you'll make is not where you work or who you party with, but who you choose to partner with for the rest of your life. Having a spouse, or life partner, whom you not only care for and want to have sex with, but who's also a good teammate, softens the rough edges, and magnifies the shine of life. I have several friends with impressive careers, wonderful friends, and a spouse they love. But they aren't happy, because their spouse isn't their partner. Their goals and approaches to life are out of sync. Misalignment on what's important and a lack of appreciation for the other person makes everything . . . harder. My friends with less economic success who spend less time with friends but who have a real partner to share their struggles and successes with are tangibly happier.

$$\heartsuit + V + \$ = P^2$$

Passion, Values, Money

The best romantic partnerships I know of are synced up on three things. They are physically attracted to each other. Sex and affection establish your relationship as singular and say "I choose you" nonverbally. Good sex is 10 percent of a relationship, but bad sex is 90 percent of a relationship. However, this is where most young people end their due diligence. You also need to ensure that you align on values like religion, how many kids you want, your approaches to raising kids, your proximity to your parents, sacrifices you're willing to make for economic success, and who handles which responsibilities. Money is an especially important value for alignment, as the number one source of marital acrimony is financial stress. Does your partner's contribution to, approach to, and expectations about money—and how it flows in and out of the household—fit with yours?

Credentials + Zip Code = Money

WE HAVE a caste system in the United States: higher education. In addition, economic growth is increasingly clustering around a handful of supercities. Two-thirds of economic growth over the next fifty years will be in supercities. Opportunity is a function of density. Get to a place that's crowded with success. Big cities are Wimbledon—even if you aren't Rafael Nadal, your game will improve by being on the court with him. And you'll either get in better shape or learn you shouldn't be at Wimbledon.

This is the peanut butter and chocolate of economic velocity. Tell me your degree (level and institution) and zip code, and I can estimate, with decent accuracy, how much money you'll make over the next decade. Advice here is simple. While you're young, get credentialed and get to a city. Both get difficult, if not impossible, as you get older. There will always be great stories about Steve Jobs, Bill Gates, and other college dropouts. Again, assume you're not that person.

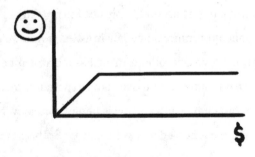

What Makes You Happy

There is a correlation between how much money you have and how happy you are. Money can buy happiness, to a point. But once you reach a certain level of economic security, the correlation flattens. More money won't make you less happy, either (also a myth). I made the mistake of spending all my time, for most of my life, trying to figure out how to make more money, instead of taking a pause and asking myself what makes me happy. So, yes, work your ass off and get some semblance of economic stability. But take notes on the things that give you joy and satisfaction, and start investing in those things. Pay special attention to things that bring you joy that don't involve mind-altering substances or a lot of money. Whether it's cooking, capoeira, the guitar, or mountain biking, interests and hobbies add texture to your personality. Being "in the zone" is happiness. You lose the sense of time, forget yourself, and feel part of something larger.

I found writing only several years ago, and it's now one of the most rewarding parts of my life. Writing is my therapy. It's a way for this shit banging around in my head to find an escape route. It's a chance to immortalize how much I love my kids, miss my mom, and love Chipotle. Writing has reconnected me with people I care about and introduced me to new, interesting people. I hope that, after I'm gone, my kids will read this stuff and feel they know me better. I wish I'd started writing thirty years ago.

Invest Early, and Often

There's an old saying that compound interest is the most powerful force in the universe. The notion of putting money away is

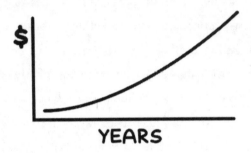

YEARS

most important to the cohort that least understand it—young people—as "long term" is not a concept they've grasped. Many talented young people assume they're so awesome that they'll make a shit-ton of money. Okay, maybe . . . but just in case it doesn't rain Benjamins, start putting away money early and often. Don't think of it as saving—think of it as magic. Put $1,000 into a magic box, and when you're ready for it in forty years, presto: that thousand dollars is now $10,000 to

$25,000. If you could have this magic box, how much would you put in it?

Most of us understand how compound interest works with money, but don't recognize its power in other parts of our lives. The app 1 Second Everyday reminds you to take a second of video each day, a small daily nuisance/investment. At the end of the year, I sit down with my kids and watch the six minutes that was our year. We watch it over and over, guessing where I was, laughing when they see themselves, remembering what a great time we had at the Wizarding World of Harry Potter.

Nothing matches the mother-child bond. It's not just instinct, but the small investments she made in you, every day, from the beginning. This can be applied to all relationships. Take a ton of pictures, text your friends stupid things, check in with old friends as often as possible, express admiration to co-workers, and every day, tell as many people as you can that you love them. A couple of minutes every day—the payoff is small at first, and then it's immense.

$$\text{💪} = R + C^{♀} + D$$

Find Your Gorilla

Feeling masculine is hugely rewarding. (I realize how strange that sounds, and that I can't really speak to the rewards of femininity.) My inner Tarzan swings on vines, and I'm happy. But the vines have changed. As a younger man, I felt masculine by impressing my friends, having sex with strange women, and being ripped. As I've gotten older, other vines have emerged. Being a loving and responsible head of household who provides for my family makes me feel "strong like bull," as does being relevant, in the classroom or at work.

Male monkeys have higher ranks and more mating success if they have more social bonds, rather than being bigger or stronger. Increasingly, being a good citizen—being a good neighbor, respecting institutions, remembering where I come from, helping people I'll never meet, taking an interest in a child who isn't mine, and voting, all stuff I never thought about when I was younger—makes me feel like beating my chest. Coming to grips with your shortcomings and making an effort to repair your deficits. In sum, being a man, and not a boy in a man's body. Masculinity now means relevance, good citizenship, and being a loving father.

 = WEALTH

Equity = Wealth

It's difficult to get to economic security with just your salary, as you will naturally raise or lower your lifestyle to match what you make. As soon as possible, buy property or stocks, and try to find a job that has forced savings through a retirement plan or, better yet, options on the firm's equity. Always be in the stock market, because you aren't smart enough to predict when to jump in and out on your own. Try not to have more than one-third of your assets in any one asset class when you're younger than forty, and lower that to 15 percent when you're older than forty.

The definition of "rich" is having passive income greater than your burn. My dad and his wife receive about $50,000 a year from dividends, pension, and Social Security, and spend $40,000 a year. They are rich. I have a number of friends who earn between $1 million and $3 million, with several children in Manhattan private schools, an ex-wife, a home in the Hamptons, and a lifestyle fitting of a master of the universe. They spend most, if not all, of it. They are poor. By the time you're thirty, you should have a feel for what your burn is. Young people are 100 percent focused on their earnings. Adults also focus on their burn.

Drink Less

The Harvard Medical School Grant Study was the largest study on happiness, tracking three hundred nineteen-year-old men for seventy-five years and looking at what factors made them less or more happy. The presence of one thing in a man's life predicted unhappiness better than any other factor: alcohol. It led to failed marriages, careers coming off the tracks, and bad health.

When I was just out of college, living in New York and working at Morgan Stanley, I'd go out every night and get shitty drunk at a very cool place with what appeared to be other successful people. It felt natural. I'm a better version of myself drunk. Drunk, I'm funny and optimistic. Sober, I'm intense and a bit boring. Also I found it near impossible to meet women unless I was fucked up (see above—swinging on vines). During the week, in the middle of the workday, I'd find myself looking for empty conference rooms so I could nurse my hangover via a thirty-minute nap under the table. Mornings were about Diet Cokes and greasy food so I could get to the afternoon when, for about an hour, I felt human again. I'd inevitably agree once more to meet a bunch of my friends from Salomon Investments and some models at the Tunnel or Limelight, where we'd order $1,200 worth of vodka, and fun Scott would show up.

Not going to class or learning much at UCLA made me a mediocre banker. However, alcohol made me a mediocre person. I'm lucky I don't have a physical addiction (I think), and when I moved to the West Coast, I didn't miss the sauce. Ask yourself, post-college, if substances are getting in the way of your relationships, professional trajectory, or life. If they are, address it.

Car < Lion

Studies show that people overestimate the amount of happiness things will bring them and underestimate the long-term positive effect of experiences. Invest in experiences over things. Drive a Hyundai, and take your wife to St. Barts.

Give Someone a Good Death

Other than my kids, the thing I am most proud of is giving my mom a good death. After my mom was diagnosed with terminal cancer, I spent seven months living with her in the Del Webb Active Adult Community in Summerlin, Nevada. During the day, I'd manage my mom's healthcare and watch *Frasier* and *Jeopardy!* with her. At night, I'd venture to the Strip and get drunk with entrepreneurs who were starting cigar bars and restaurants, and strippers. It was a strange but meaningful time in my life. The instinctive rewards from nurturing people at the beginning of life—the joy of children—are well documented. However, providing comfort for someone you love at the end of their life is also deeply satisfying. If you're in a position—and many aren't—to make a loved one's exit more graceful, do it—you'll cherish the experience for the rest of your life.

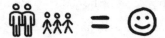

Happiness = Family

On a balanced scorecard, the happiest people are those in monogamous relationships who have children. I didn't want to get married or have children, and I still don't believe you need children be happy. I can say, however, that being a decent dad and raising kids with someone I love and who's competent has, for the first time, begun to address the question we all struggle with: Why am I here?

$$R/F = S$$

Resilience / Failure = Success

Everyone experiences failure and tragedy. You will get fired, lose people you love, and likely have periods of economic stress. The key to success is the ability to mourn and then move on. I've had a marriage fail, had businesses go bankrupt, and lost the only person who (at that point) I knew loved me, my mom . . . all before I was forty. But blessed with a great education, good friends, some talent, and the best zip code in the world (USA), these were obstacles for me, not barriers.

Nothing Is Ever As Bad or As Good As It Seems

As my friend Todd Benson says, market dynamics trump individual performance. Your successes and failures aren't entirely your fault. The number one piece of advice seniors would give to their younger selves is that they wish they'd been less hard on themselves. Our competitive instincts lead us to anchor off the most successful people we know, and we're disappointed when the person in the mirror doesn't match those achievements.

One of the keys to a healthy relationship is forgiveness, as you, and your partner, will at some point screw up. Your limited time here mandates that you hold yourself accountable. But also be ready to forgive yourself so you can get on with the important business of life.

$$\text{PERCEIVED} \downarrow \ < \ \text{REAL} \downarrow$$

$$\text{PERCEIVED} \uparrow \ < \ \text{REAL} \uparrow$$

Success

The following are (true) short stories about my upbringing and how I developed a tool kit for success and economic security.

Stay Thirsty

I THINK a lot about success and its underpinnings. Talent is key, but it will only gain you entrance to a crowded VIP room. Kind of like Platinum Medallion on Delta: you think you're special, but at LaGuardia, you realize there are a lot of you. Let's assume you are exceptionally talented. Maybe even in the top 1 percent. Congrats: you join 75 million people, the population of Germany, all vying for more than their share of the world's resources. When I ask young adults to describe the life they aspire to, most of them outline an environment and accoutrements that are the ecosystem of a cohort that contains millions. Or to put it another way, most young people reading this book likely aspire to be in the top .1 percent. And talent alone won't get you within spitting distance of .1 percent.

The chaser that takes talent over the top into success is hunger. Hunger can come from a lot of places. I don't think I was born with it. I have a great deal of insecurity and fear, which, coupled with the instincts we all have, has resulted in hunger. Understanding where hunger comes from can illuminate the difference between success and fulfillment.

For the first eighteen years of my life, I didn't work hard. At UCLA, we all started as nice, smart, attractive people ("eighteen" and "attractive" are redundant), who had crushes on each other based on a clumsy sense of attraction ("she's hot" / "he's cool"). But by senior year, the women were gravitating toward guys who had their shit together, showed early signs of success, or having rich parents, already had the trappings of success, like weekends at their parents' pads in Aspen or Palm Springs.

The women's instincts were kicking in, and they were seeking out mates who could better ensure their offspring's survival—instead of crushing on a funny guy who wore a thin leather tie with Top-Siders and could recite key scenes from the Planet of the Apes trilogy. My instincts were also kicking in, and I wanted to increase my selection set of mates. I decided a requisite for this was to signal success, so I landed a job at Morgan Stanley. I had no idea what investment bankers did, but I knew being one signaled success.

It didn't take long to realize that the secret is to find something you're good at. The rewards and recognition that stem from being great at something will make you passionate about whatever that something is. Investment banking, for me, was a unique combination of boring subject matter and a great deal of stress. Figuring out early that my hunger to impress was leading down a road of misery gave me the confidence to get out. I quit the path of success devoid of fulfillment.

The second event also involved the female sex. In my second year of grad school, my mother was diagnosed with an aggressive form of breast cancer. Prematurely discharged from Kaiser Permanente hospital in Los Angeles, she started chemo. She called me at Berkeley and said she was feeling awful. I flew home that afternoon and walked through the door into our dark living room. My mom was lying on the couch, in her robe, contorted and vomiting into a trash can, distraught. She looked at me and asked, "What are we going to do?" It rattles me just to write this.

We were underinsured, and I didn't have any contacts who were doctors. I felt a rush of emotions, but mostly I wished I had more money and influence. I knew that wealth, among other things, brought contacts and access to a different level of healthcare. We had neither.

Nausea

In 2008, my girlfriend got pregnant, and I witnessed the profoundly disturbing miracle of birth as my son rotated out of her. Note: I still think men should be out of the room. I felt pretty much none of the things you're supposed to feel: love, gratitude, wonder. Mostly nausea and panic at the science experiment we were embarking on to keep this thing alive. However, as it often does, instinct kicked in, and the experiment became less awful, even likable. The need to protect and provide grew increasingly intense.

When the 2008 financial crisis hit, it hit me hard. I went from sort of wealthy to most definitely not. The previous crisis, in 2000, had registered the same economic effect, but it had rolled right off me, as I was in my early thirties and knew I could take care of myself. But this was different. Not being able to provide for the needs of a kid in Manhattan at the level and texture I envisioned for my son seriously fucked with my sense of why I was here (as in, on Earth) and my worth as a man. I was shaping up to fail on a cosmic level, and the flame of hunger burned brighter.

The pressure many of us put on ourselves to be a good provider is irrational. The instinct to protect and nurture your offspring is core to the success of our species. However, believing that your kid must have Manhattan private schools and a loft in Tribeca is your ego, not paternal instincts. You can be a good, even great, dad on a lot less than I thought I needed to earn. Nonetheless, I felt deficient.

Lately I feel my hunger changing complexion. More a pursuit of relevance, versus money. I'm spending more time with people and projects I care about, at the expense of earning money. Trying to be more in the moment, and passing on certain economic opportunities so I can do more stuff focused on the condition of my soul. I'm also trying to instill a sense of hunger in my boys via chores. I'm paying them each week for their tasks, hoping they will connect work with reward and get hungry. Also, twice a year after paying them, I mug them (tackle them and steal their money) on the way to their room, as that, too, is a life lesson.

Embrace Adulthood

EVERY SPRING, SoHo is mobbed by purple ghosts—twenty-two-year-olds in NYU caps and gowns. Close in tow are typically a man and woman who look similar to the twenty-two-year-old, but older and heavier, beaming with pride. Commencement season is nice, even hopeful. This moment is more rewarding for the heavier versions of you (your parents), as your graduation is a testament to their success (getting you to and through college). They can check the last evolutionary box they're responsible for . . . other than dying (ughhh, that sounded awful).

Neither of my graduations was that joyous. At UCLA, I graduated midway through my fifth year, with most of my friends gone, as they had done it in the prescribed four years. I spent most of my last two weeks at UCLA asking professors to change an F to a D so I could get credits for the course and graduate, as I was three courses shy of a BS in economics. My pitch was simple and rang true:

- **"I live with my mother in an upper-lower-middle-class home."**
- **"I have a great job offer from Morgan Stanley in New York."**
- **"The sooner I'm out of here, the sooner you can let in someone more deserving."**

I asked four profs (and there were more I could have asked). Three had the same reaction: they looked at me with disgust, then resignation, signed the form, and asked me to leave their office. No robe and very little pomp and circumstance.

My second graduation, from Berkeley, was more rewarding, as I had gotten my act together, or something, and earned my MBA. I was selected to be the student speaker at commencement and remember looking up, mid-speech, and seeing my mom, cancer marching through her, amid a sea of thousands of parents sitting in the glaring sun at Berkeley's Greek Theatre. She was standing, as she couldn't maintain her pride, waving at me with both hands.

I don't believe in an afterlife, but I plan to indulge in a lot of psilocybin before I check out, as I'd like to have some of the bright-light visions people describe when they are near death. I expect/hope I will see two visions: one of my kids rolling on top of me in bed, laughing, and the image of my mom standing and waving as if she needs to remind me she's there, and that she is my mother.

Still, it was an insecure time . . . as it is for a lot of kids. A twenty-six-year-old male is still very much a kid. I had a sick parent and turned down an offer from a consulting firm so I could start my own consulting firm. The ballast in my life was my girlfriend, who provided emotional and financial security. She had a real job.

It is by now a cliché for writers to use graduation as a chance to talk about themselves, in the third person, with Vaseline smeared over the filter they want you to view their past through. But if I *were* to give advice to any newly minted grads, it'd go something like this . . .

Don't Follow Your Passion

People who speak at universities, especially at commencement, who tell you to follow your passion—or my favorite, to "never

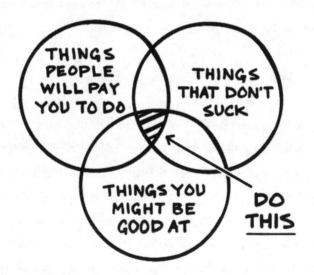

give up"—are already rich. And most got there by starting waste treatment plants after failing at five other ventures—that is, they knew when to give up. Your job is to find something you're good at, and after ten thousand hours of practice, get great at it. The emotional and economic rewards that accompany being great at something will make you passionate about whatever that something is. Nobody starts their career passionate about tax law. But great tax lawyers are passionate about colleagues who admire them, creating economic security for their families, and marrying someone more impressive than they are.

Boring Is Sexy

Careers are asset classes. If a sector becomes overinvested with human capital, the returns on those efforts are suppressed. If you want to work at *Vogue*, produce movies, or open a restaurant, you need to ensure that you receive a great deal of psychic income, as the returns on your efforts (distinct of well-publicized exceptions) will be, on a risk-adjusted basis, awful. I try to avoid investing in anything that sounds remotely cool.

I didn't buy *BlackBook* magazine, or invest in Ford Models or a downtown members-only club focused on music. If, on the other hand, the business, and the issue the business addresses, sounds so boring I want to put a gun in my mouth, then . . . bingo, I'll invest. I recently spoke at the J.P. Morgan Alternative Investment Summit, where the bank hosts three hundred of the wealthiest families in the world. There are some who own media properties or a national airline, but most killed it in iron/ore smelting, insurance, or pesticides.

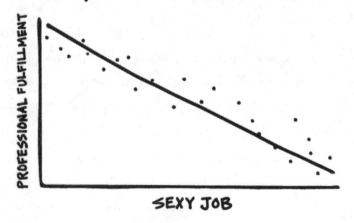

PROF. GALLOWAY CAREER ADVICE

PROFESSIONAL FULFILLMENT

SEXY JOB

The Adult in the Room

YOUR ROLE vis-à-vis your parents will reverse. They become the child and you the parent. It usually happens organically. However, graduation is a decent time to expedite the transition. Your actions need to begin saying "I got this" to your parents as you become a source of solutions versus stress. It shocks me how many people are the adults in the room until they get around their parents and regress into whiny children expecting their parents to solve their problems. The most rewarding things in life are rooted in instinct. We give a lot of airtime to how rewarding it is to raise kids. What gets less attention is how rewarding it is to help take care of your parents. Start now.

Getting the Easy Stuff Right, and Email

I'VE STRUGGLED my whole career with getting the easy stuff right. I'll rally a team to pull together an insightful, hard-hitting presentation and then show up to that presentation fifteen minutes late, pissing everyone off. After the meeting, I'll get an email from the client about additional work, or some other opportunity, then not respond in a timely fashion and lose momentum. I don't follow up with people when I should. In general, a lack of professionalism and bad manners has reduced the slope of my trajectory. Strange, as I know when I'm doing it, and I know how to fix it . . . and still don't.

The lesson here . . . easy: don't be a fucking idiot like yours truly, and get the easy stuff right.

- **Show up early.**
- **Have good manners.**
- **Follow up.**

I believe most people are especially repelled by attributes in other people that remind them of things they loathe about themselves. The following story, about an email, was my first brush with internet fame. In sum, a student was late to class, I kicked him out, and some drama ensued (our email exchange was forwarded to the press). One article on the exchange garnered 700,000 views and 305 comments. At one point,

according to the dean's office at NYU Stern, they were receiving an email (regarding the email) every two minutes. Most were supportive, some were not . . . at all ("I'm not letting my son register at NYU this fall"). The exchange is now a static part of my course outline. I'm fairly certain this is the most-read "late policy" in the history of academia.

The Email I Received:

From: xxxx@stern.nyu.edu
To: xxxx@stern.nyu.edu
Sent: Tuesday, February 9, 2010 7:15:11 PM
Subject: Brand Strategy Feedback

Prof. Galloway,

I would like to discuss a matter with you that bothered me. Yesterday evening I entered your 6pm Brand Strategy class approximately 1 hour late. As I entered the room, you quickly dismissed me, saying that I would need to leave and come back to the next class. After speaking with several students who are taking your class, they explained that you have a policy stating that students who arrive more than 15 minutes late will not be admitted to class.

As of yesterday evening, I was interested in three different Monday night classes that all occurred simultaneously. In order to decide which class to select, my plan for the evening was to sample all three and see which one I like most. Since I had never taken your class, I was unaware of your class policy. I was disappointed that you dismissed me from class considering (1) there is no way I could have been aware of your policy and (2) considering that it was the first day of evening classes and I arrived 1 hour late (not a few minutes), it was more probable that my tardiness was due to my desire to sample different classes rather than sheer complacency.

I have already registered for another class but I just wanted to be open and provide my opinion on the matter.

Regards,

xxxx

—

xxxx

MBA 2010 Candidate

NYU Stern School of Business

xxxx@stern.nyu.edu

xxx-xxx-xxxx

My Reply:

From: xxxx@stern.nyu.edu

To: xxxx@stern.nyu.edu

Sent: Tuesday, February 9, 2010 9:34:02 PM GMT

Subject: Re: Brand Strategy Feedback

xxxx:

Thanks for the feedback. I, too, would like to offer some
feedback.

Just so I've got this straight . . . you started in one class, left 15–20 minutes into it (stood up, walked out mid-lecture), went to another class (walked in 20 minutes late), left that class (again, presumably, in the middle of the lecture), and then came to my class. At that point (walking in an hour late), I asked you to come to the next class which "bothered" you.

Correct?

You state that, having not taken my class, it would be impossible to know our policy of not allowing people to walk in an hour late. Most risk analysis offers that in the face of substantial uncertainty, you opt for the more conservative path or hedge your bet (e.g., do not show up an hour late until you know the professor has an explicit policy for tolerating disrespectful behavior, check with the TA before class, etc.). I hope the lottery winner that is your recently crowned Monday-evening professor is teaching Judgment and Decision-Making or Critical Thinking.

In addition, your logic effectively means you cannot be held accountable for any code of conduct before taking a class. For the record, we also have no stated policy against bursting into show tunes in the middle of class, urinating on desks, or taking that revolutionary hair-removal system for a spin. However, xxxx, there is a baseline level of decorum (i.e., manners) that we expect of grown men and women who the admissions department have deemed tomorrow's business leaders.

xxxx, let me be more serious for a moment. I do not know you, will not know you, and have no real affinity or animosity for you. You are an anonymous student who is now regretting the send button on his laptop. It's within this context that I hope you register pause . . . REAL pause, xxxx, and take to heart what I am about to tell you:

xxxx, get your shit together.

Getting a good job, working long hours, keeping your skills relevant, navigating the politics of an organization, finding a work-life balance . . . these are all really hard, xxxx. In contrast, respecting institutions, having manners, demonstrating a level of humility . . . these are all (relatively) easy. Get the easy stuff right, xxxx. In and of themselves, they will not make you successful. However, not possessing them will hold you back, and you will not achieve your potential, which, by virtue of you being admitted to Stern, you must have in spades. It's not too late, xxxx . . .

Again, thanks for the feedback.

Professor Galloway

Believe You Deserve It

IN 1982, Emerson Junior High School, in its ninth-grade poll, named me "Most Comical" and "Steve Martin." Since then I've successfully navigated all awards and recognition. A month ago a friend, Anne Maffei, texted me, "Please respond to my brother, he wants to give you an award that recognizes your work."

Huh?

Anne's brother is Greg Maffei, CEO of Liberty Media, a mass media firm founded by the original gangster of cable, John Malone (#badass). Before that, Greg was CFO of Microsoft . . . which feels even more gangster/uber-cool to me. I think being CFO of the evil empire of the nineties is as close to Darth Vader of the corporate world as one can get. But Greg is too likable to be the Dark Lord, so I envision him as Darth Vader after he defeats the emperor, removes his mask, and returns from the dark side.

So, a quick search of my inbox and there they are: emails from Greg and his colleagues congratulating me as the 2018 recipient of the Media for Liberty Award. I had been gracious enough to ignore them for two months. Liberty, five years ago, crafted an award for an author or journalist who writes about the intersection of politics and the economy. I'm pretty sure Greg is a billionaire, as all the elected officials at the event were really, really nice to him (see above: CFO of Microsoft in the nineties), and I think it's fitting that a professor was too out-to-lunch to respond. So I got back to Greg ("Yes, this is awesome . . . thanks") and agreed to accept the award at a ceremony in DC over dinner and drinks at the Newseum—"DC's favorite museum" in 2016, according to the *Washingtonian*.

I am excited about the day, but anxious/uneasy. I'm nervous that I'm flying too close to the sun. That, in sum:

I'm. A. Fraud.

Increased attention/recognition puts a guy on my shoulder whispering in my ear, "Who are you kidding? You're a fraud." Whenever success came my way, it was because I was "fooling them." I didn't warrant recognition as an academic, nor rewards as an entrepreneur. I felt an anxiety, always, that I'd be

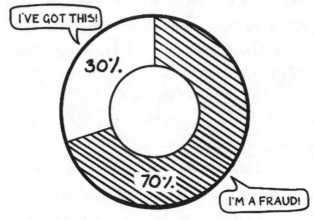

AMERICANS WITH IMPOSTOR SYNDROME

I'VE GOT THIS!

30%.

70%.

I'M A FRAUD!

SOURCE: NBC NEWS, 2017.

found out for what I really am: the son of a secretary, who did poorly in school, did not invest in relationships, was selfish, and isn't that gifted. Someone whose only real talent was self-promotion and taking credit for other people's work. A fraud.

The anxiety is sort of dissipating as I realize that most successful people reach beyond their grasp. Seventy percent of Americans admit to experiencing impostor syndrome. Unless you take time to squash these thoughts, they get louder, psychologists say. So I cut myself some slack, as there's been some hard work, risk, and giving along the way.

Still, there's always the insecurity whispering in my ear—*I know who you really are.* I hope this is insecurity, not common sense or clarity.

Anxious Scott Goes to Washington

The dinner and award ceremony were wonderful. Overlooking the Capitol, reflecting on the day, I loved being American. Despite the voice on my shoulder, I summoned the skills to present well during the conversation with Greg . . . who is great at helping others be better at what they do. I had friends in the audience ranging from my best friend from the fourth grade to new friends from Florida and a dozen in between. Like many important events, there were moments of melancholy. I wish my mom could have seen me. I wish my dad was well enough to have been there. I have a good friend who attended whose husband is very sick, and I could feel some of the weight and sadness she was bearing, and how generous it was of her to be there. I also felt the love of friends and of my wife, who rode on planes and trains for six hours to cement this moment for me. Achievement is just a moment in pencil unless you can share it with people you care about. Then it becomes real, a memory in permanent ink. The voice of insecurity is still on my shoulder. However, it dims as I feel American, relevant, and loved.

Find Your Voice

WHEN I was around five, I noticed that people behaved differently around my father. They would gaze into his eyes, nodding and then laughing. Women would touch his arm, laughing, and men, when they saw him, would yell, "Tommy," genuinely happy to see him. He was great with a turn of phrase, funny and clever (i.e., British). The cocktail of articulate, irreverent, and smart chased with a Scottish accent made my dad attractive to women and employers.

My mother explained it to me: "Your father is charming." At gatherings, inevitably, a semicircle forms around my dad, and he tells jokes and shares his take on things ranging from space ("if it never ends, everything has already happened") to management ("the key is a good job description"). This charm sustained, for a decade, an upper-middle-class lifestyle for him, my mom, and me as he roamed the western United States and Canada, maintaining, in fifteen-minute spurts, pseudo-friendships with the managers of the outdoor and garden departments at Sears and Lowe's. In exchange for his company, my dad's two hundred friends would over-order bags of shit . . . as he was selling fertilizer from O.M. Scotts & Sons, an International Telegraph and Telegram (ITT) company.

In his late fifties, after the marketplace made it clear a recently laid-off middle manager from ITT was no longer welcome in the Fortune 500, he began giving seminars, open to the public, at a local community college. Cheap fluorescent lighting made the space feel like an operating room in an East German hospital. There were six rows of eight folding chairs, an overhead slide projector, transparencies with smudges, and a table at the back with half-empty two-liter bottles of Dr Pepper, Sprite, and Tab, and lemon squares my stepmom had baked. Around fifteen people, most in their fifties and sixties, would attend. My dad would speak for ninety minutes, breaking halfway through so everyone could venture to the hall and have a cigarette. I attended a few times as a teen. At that age, I found everything involving my parents lame, but this felt especially sad . . . depressing, even. In exchange for imparting his wisdom on other mostly unemployed smokers, my dad had to pay $10 to $20 for gas and treats.

My dad reflects on these seminars as the happiest he's ever been. He was where he was meant to be, in front of a group of people, speaking and teaching.

Charm Skips a Generation

I did not inherit my father's charm. In fact, being offensive—the opposite of charm—is something I've developed a knack for. Not a "speak truth to power" kind of offensive, but a tone-deaf "saying exactly the wrong thing at the exact wrong moment" kind of offensive. I regularly say things and write emails that make good people feel bad, and I know it. No excuse. Because I'm successful, people often recast this offensiveness as honesty or even leadership. No, it's just being an asshole. I'm working on it.

However, my father did pass on the ability to hold a room of people, as long as it's a windowless boardroom or conference hall on the fifty-fifth floor of a Midtown building or in the basement of a hotel. Most people become increasingly uncomfortable as the group grows. I experience the inverse. One-on-one, I'm an introvert, insecure even. But as the room fills . . . other skills kick in. In front of dozens, crisp insights find me. In front of hundreds, humor and warmth. And thousands, a rush of adrenaline and the confidence to reach beyond my grasp and be inspiring. I may be wrong, but my heart is in the right place. I can look each person in the eye and assert I believe what I'm saying to be true.

Stand-Up

To hone their craft, comedians do stand-up at clubs. For me, stand-up is class, where I hone the craft of speaking every Tuesday night for three hours in front of 170 second-year MBAs. I'm much more focused, and put more effort into the class, than in front of any board or gathering of gold-circle commercial real estate brokers. I make much less, about $1,000, per podium hour. (Note: This sounds like more than it is, as you spend several hours outside of class prepping or meeting with students for each podium hour.) In addition, the amount of bullshit you endure to get to this platform—advanced degrees, department politics—is substantial.

Two Things

My dad will only get on a plane for two things, and they aren't to see his grandkids or spend time with friends. He will only get on a plane to see the Toronto Maple Leafs play or to watch his son teach. He sits in the back row of the classroom. At the beginning of class, we ask any visitors to introduce themselves—we get half a dozen curious undergrads or applicants in almost every class. My dad waits until they're done and then, really dialing up the accent, says:

"I'm Tom Galloway, Scott's father."

There's a pause, then sustained applause. I see my dad riveted on my every word and movement for the next three hours. I wonder if, at eighty-eight, he looks at me and feels disappointment he didn't have the opportunities to reach his full potential as a speaker, or if he feels the reward of evolutionary progress, seeing himself, but version 2.0. Seeing my dad in class reminds me that the difference between bribing people to listen to you with lemon squares and being paid $2,000 per minute at corporate gatherings is not talent—my dad has more of that. The difference is being born in America, and the generosity of California taxpayers, who gave the child of a secretary the chance to attend a world-class university. The mix of my dad's talent and the confidence I got from the abundant love of his second wife gave me the skills and opportunity to stand in front of a room full of people, look each in the eyes, and say, "I believe this to be true."

Know Your Worth

The wind of our society's obsession with big tech is at my back, running over my vocal cords. My domain of expertise, big tech, is white-hot, and the economy is strong. These skills, coupled with proprietary data that dozens of overeducated twenty-somethings at L2 collect and distill into insight, and a world-class creative team that designs imagery and charts, shot on the screen behind me, all sing like Pavarotti.

My market value, like all things, will fade. People will tire of my topics, and I won't have access to the resources that make my stuff great, versus just good. Or more likely, my creative juices will just stop flowing. Working with young, creative people and having access to the best and brightest thinkers in business is for me what heroin was to Ray Charles. Once it's gone, no more hits.

My relationship with NYU, generally speaking: I teach a mess of kids and speak at events. In exchange, they put up with me. Every three or four years a new department chair or administrator asks me to teach more, changes my status, or does something to piss me off. I threaten to go to Wharton or Cornell Tech, and I mostly get what I want. If I sound like a diva or a pain in the ass, trust your instincts. I don't act like an employee at Stern, but a free agent, and it frustrates them. My star is burning bright right now—I'm good at teaching and I strengthen the Stern brand, so they tolerate me. But when my value begins to wane (and it's only a matter of time), they'll drop me like second-period French. I would.

You Are (Probably) Not Mark Zuckerberg

THE TRAITS of successful entrepreneurs haven't changed much in the digital age: you need more builders than branders, and it's key to have a technologist as part of, or near, the founding team. But there are four tests or questions:

1. Can you sign the front, not the back, of checks?
2. Are you comfortable with public failure?
3. Do you like to sell?
4. How risk aggressive are you?

Can You Sign the Front, and Not the Back, of Checks?

I know people who have all the skills to build great businesses. But they'll never do so, because they could never go to work only to, at the end of the month, in exchange for working eighty hours a week, write the firm a check.

Unless you've built firms and shepherded them to successful exits, or have access to seed capital (most don't, and it's always expensive), then you'll need to pay the company for the right to work your ass off until you can raise money. And most start-ups never raise the needed money. Most people can't wrap their heads around the notion of working without getting paid—and 99-plus percent will never risk their own capital for the pleasure of . . . working.

Are You Comfortable with Public Failure?

Most failures are private: you decide law school isn't for you (bombed the LSAT), to spend more time with your kids (got fired), or to work on "projects" (can't get a job). However, there's no hiding your own business failure. It's you, and if you're so awesome, your business must succeed . . . right? Wrong, and when it doesn't, it feels like elementary school, where the marketplace is a sixth grader laughing at you because you've wet your pants . . . times a hundred.

Do You Like to Sell?

The word "entrepreneur" is a synonym for "salesperson." Selling people to join your firm, selling them to stay at your firm, selling investors, and (oh yeah) selling customers. It doesn't matter if you're running the corner store or Pinterest—you'd better be damn good at selling if you plan to start a business. Selling is calling people who don't want to hear from you, pretending to like them, getting treated poorly, and then calling them again. I likely won't start another business because my ego is getting too big to sell. I, incorrectly, believe our collective genius at L2 should mean the product sells itself, and sometimes it does. There has to be a product that doesn't require you to get out the spoon and publicly eat shit over and over. Actually, no, there isn't.

Google has an algorithm that can answer anything and identify people who have explicitly declared an interest in buying your product, then advertise to those people at that exact moment. Yet Google still has to hire thousands of attractive people with average IQs and exceptional EQ to sell the shit out of . . . Google. Entrepreneurship is a sales job with negative commissions until you raise capital, are profitable, or go out of business—whichever comes first.

The good news: If you like to sell and are good at it, you'll always make more money, relative to how hard you work, than any of your colleagues, and . . . they'll hate you for it.

How Risk Aggressive Are You?

Being successful in a big firm isn't easy, and it requires a unique skill set. You have to play nice with others, suffer injustices and bullshit at every turn, and be politically savvy—get noticed by key stakeholders doing good work and garner executive-level sponsorship. However, if you're good at working at a big firm, then, on a risk-adjusted basis, you are better off doing just that—and not struggling against the long odds facing a small firm. For me, entrepreneurship was a survival mechanism, as I didn't have the skills to be successful in the greatest platforms for economic success in history, big US companies.

With the endless and well-publicized stories of billionaire college dropouts, we romanticize entrepreneurship. Ask yourself, and some people you trust, the preceding questions about your personality and skills. If you answer positively on the first two, and you're not skilled at working at a big company, then step into the cage of chaos monkeys.

When to Take Cover

IN 1999, I and a gaggle of other San Francisco internet founders and CEOs went to an airfield where we browsed private jets. It made sense that, at thirty-four, I should have a one-bedroom apartment to transport me across the surface of the atmosphere at Mach .8, because I was a fucking genius who could afford, on paper, to spend the equivalent of a thousand years of my mother's salary on a Gulfstream.

A bunch of thirtysomething dicks looking at planes, and it feeling normal, is a decent signal that the canary is dying, and these budding masters of the universe are about to get bitch-slapped—which we were. I never got the jet. But I've achieved Mosaic status on JetBlue.

Jamie Dimon, CEO of JPMorgan Chase, defines a financial crisis as "something that happens every five to seven years." It's been eleven since the last recession. As you get old enough to observe cycles as actual cycles, you begin to recognize that the economic time you're in is a point on a curved line and, sooner than you think, the direction of the line will change. Better or worse.

An asset bubble is a wave of optimism that lifts prices beyond levels warranted by fundamentals, ending in a crash. In 1999, I promised myself that I'd be smarter the next time. "Next time" meaning on the cusp of a pop or recession.

So how do you ID when we've entered the danger zone, and should you adjust your behavior? There are several hard metrics for why we may be nearing a full-monty bubble, including things my NYU colleagues spend a great deal of time thinking about, and understand much better. But you don't need a Nobel to see the similarities between 1999 and 2019. Some of the softer metrics are far better canaries in this particular coal mine.

Signs that markets or a company are about to find themselves on the wrong side of cyclicality

- **The metrics around valuations, P/E ratios, and easy credit-inflating bubbles are logical indicators of dead**

canaries. Seth Klarman, the most successful hedge fund manager nobody's heard of, warned recently that the sugar high of stimulus combined with high-cholesterol protectionism doesn't end well.

- **When nations and firms start erecting big buildings, look out.** The Pan Am Building, Sears Tower, and any number of giant penises plunging into Mother Earth in emerging markets are little more than multibillion-dollar dick pics and may seem like a good idea at the time, but are just tacky.

- **The most obvious doomed canaries within companies are typically manifestations of the CEO's ego.** The strongest sell signals are when the CEO goes Hollywood, or believes the world shouldn't suffer their absence from fashion covers and ads. David Karp in J. Crew ads and Dennis Crowley in Gap ads should have told us their companies would soon be shadows of their former selves and valuations. Marissa Mayer's 3,000-word profile in the September issue of *Vogue* around the time she spent $3 million of shareholder money sponsoring *Vogue*'s Met Ball was an indicator of poor judgment. This way of thinking leads you to spend another billion dollars of shareholder money to purchase the blog platform (Tumblr) of the guy who's in the J. Crew ads, only to find you spent $1.1 billion on a porn site that has little revenue.

- **A CEO's fashion can also be telling.** When he or she starts showing up onstage wearing a black turtleneck ("I'm the next Steve Jobs"), it likely means not that Jobs has reincarnated, but that the company's stock is about to crash (Jack Dorsey) and/or that the FDA is going to ban you from your own labs (Elizabeth Holmes).

- **Mediocrity + two years' tech experience = six figures.** Kids who can code and are two years out of school, who are mediocre, are making $100,000+ in the market. What's worse is that they believe they're worth it. If you can code, yay for you. But you have no real hard skills or management ability. Not recognizing that you're over-paid means you won't have the funds to avoid your parents' basement when shit gets real.

- **Bidding wars for commercial real estate.** Firms that investors believe are the next Google, armed with cheap capital, roam the streets of New York and San Francisco, driving up commercial real estate. They are also competing with the Four (Amazon, Apple, Facebook, and Google), who are purchasing superblocks in NYC.

- **Gross idolatry of youth.** I was invited to the World Economic Forum's annual meeting in Davos when I was thirty-two, pre-crisis, as internet entrepreneurs were the new masters of the universe. I met with several CEOs who wanted insight from me on business, as clearly I had unique insight. No, I didn't. I was a reasonably talented thirty-two-year-old, who at any other time would have been making only a decent living. Instead, I was Yoda,

lecturing more talented businesspeople on what their firms should do. When the dot.bomb hit, I was thirty-four and returned to Davos, where I couldn't get arrested—nobody would meet with me.

When times are bad, people look to gray hair for leadership. When times are good/frothy, people look for youth. Evan Spiegel and Jack Dorsey are incredibly talented young men who have built companies that are likely worth hundreds of millions, maybe even a billion dollars, but not tens of billions. Snap, WeWork, Uber, Twitter—combined, worth more than Boeing—are run by talented young men who in their next lives will be vice presidents (optimistic) and really grateful. As a former twentysomething CEO of new-economy firms, I can tell you that the greatest asset of a child CEO is being too stupid to know you're going to fail. Young CEOs pursue avenues that are crazy and that sometimes end up being crazy-genius. But most are just too inexperienced to be running companies that hundreds or thousands of families depend on for their livelihood.

If the tech boom continues its run, there's a non-zero probability a teenager will be the founder/CEO of a $1 billion-value tech firm in the next decade. When that happens, we really will be on the precipice of the economic zombie apocalypse. If he or she wears a black turtleneck, treats employees like shit, and sports tattoos, a nose ring, or other accouterments of youth, society will treat them like Jesus Christ. We now worship at the altar of innovation and youth, versus character or kindness.

What to Do If You Think You Might Be in a Bubble

I'VE FOUNDED, or cofounded, nine firms. The factor most strongly correlated to success or failure? When they were started. The successful firms were launched as we were coming out of recessions (1992 and 2009). People, real estate, and services are all much less expensive. My chief strategy officer at L2 joined us in 2009, and she has been the secret sauce of our success, as her offer from a consulting firm was delayed (see: recession), and my offer of $10 per hour was her best option. (Note: She makes substantially more now.)

Companies started in boom times (1998, 2006) struggled. The people our firms have been able to attract in boom times were mediocre, as great people were killing it elsewhere. In addition, cheap capital served as a hallucinogen for the viability of our products and services in the marketplace. Right now, stick with a big company that, if you're good, believes you'll leave for Squarespace if they don't pay you well. If you're a start-up (or any firm, for that matter), raise money as if you won't be able to for a while. If you're raising $1 million, raise $5 million. In general, you want to raise money when you don't need to. Don't go to business school (unless it's NYU, of course). Business school has become the domain of the elite and the aimless, or a place to take refuge from a recession. If you're doing well at a good firm during a boom time, stay put.

It remains to be seen how all this will play out, but if you suspect the crash is around the corner, here are some ideas.

Know When to Sell

In 2017, convinced we were on the precipice of a bubble popping, I sold. Or at least I sold assets I didn't expect or want to own for at least ten years. If you're young, your money in the market can survive gyrations (it's difficult to time the market). But if you're an entrepreneur or find yourself sitting on assets that represent a large portion of your wealth, I'm comfortable saying that while a bull market may not be the best time to sell, it's most certainly not a bad time to sell. We sold L2 in 2017. I was confident about the firm's prospects, but market dynamics trump individual performance. We were eight years into a bull market and due, even overdue, for a correction.

Despite well-publicized examples of people who made billions with extreme concentration of their wealth (think Bezos, Gates, and Zuckerberg), assume you will not be one of these people. Pursue one of the truisms of investing and accreting wealth: diversification. If you're fortunate to have one asset, be it a stock or a house, run up so dramatically that it represents the vast majority of your wealth, get as much of that asset liquid as possible. If there is pressure not to sell, ask yourself if the people (board, investors, market, media) pressuring you are already rich, and if they are, ignore them. Most times when I've had a substantial run-up in one of my assets (usually stock in one of my companies) and not pursued liquidity, the market steps in and diversifies for me via a crash in the value of my company. *You*, not the market, should be the arbiter of diversification of your assets.

Cash

I'm 80 percent in cash, which most reasonable financial managers will tell you is stupid. Even if it's stupid, it doesn't get near the medals podium of stupid things I've done (like, at thirty-two, turning down $55 million for my first firm, which was doing $4 million in revenues; being 100 percent in tech stocks, etc.). So, there's that. Every time the bubble popped, I wished I had dry powder and lots of it as the market became the anti-corollary to Snap—good companies at low valuations (Williams-Sonoma at $5 per share, Apple at $12, etc.). I'm willing to give up gains, as I so badly want to be on the right side of the street when the recession hits this time.

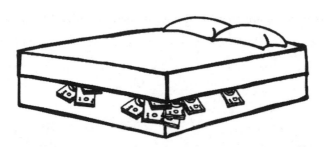

Smart financial advisers will tell you to always be in the market. I just can't help it . . . mattress time.

Be Humble

It's key, if you're doing really well, to realize that much of it isn't your fault—you've been swept up in a boom. This humility will result in your living within your means and will prepare you financially and psychologically for the next card you're dealt. And when the next part of the cycle shows up—and it will—you can take solace knowing (again) it's not your fault, and you aren't the idiot the market might make you feel you are.

Measure What Matters

IT'S INSTINCTUAL to "manage to the test." The metrics we value are the guardrails of our intentions, actions, and values. We all have an internal Fitbit/Apple Watch, trying to hit certain metrics in different areas of life. Your metrics, and the numbers that loom large for you, say a lot about who you are. The metrics that are never far for me—good, bad, and ugly:

Net worth. I think about money a lot. I realize how awful that sounds. When I didn't have much of it, I didn't track it. And even now, when I know my portfolio has been beaten up, I don't check my brokerage accounts for a few days, as I don't want to get bummed out and I know that (most of the time) they'll recover. Like most things in life, your gains and losses in the market are never as good or bad as they seem. I'd much rather work in private equity or venture capital than for a hedge fund, as having a scorecard every day is just plain stressful.

Wealthy people claim they don't think much about money. That's bullshit—they are obsessed with money. The notion that rich people don't think about money is an attempt to dampen resentment (e.g., revolution) from the 3.5 billion people who have fewer assets than the wealthiest twelve individuals. What, like, rich people got there because they are just so benign and talented, it just happened ("oops, I'm rich")? As I've said before, people who tell you to follow your passion are already rich. They have doggedly pursued a path and have been obsessed with success for a long time. They want to sound inspirational and give you a sound bite, because the truth that success requires sixty- to eighty-hour weeks for several decades doesn't get applause in graduation speeches.

Every wealthy person I've known measures their net worth in frightening detail, and measures it often. You have to stay nimble, or you stand to lose a lot. We live in a capitalist society, and the amount of money you have is a forward-looking indicator of the effectiveness of your healthcare, the comfort of your home, the harmony of your relationships, and the quality of your children's education.

580. In my late twenties, I had trouble getting a mortgage for my first home out of college, as my credit score was 580. It wasn't that I didn't make money, but I was too irresponsible/ immature/stupid to pay my bills on time. I've always felt I have a big "580" sign above my head.

120K and 350K. My Twitter following and the average number of views my YouTube series Winners & Losers used to get each week, respectively. (We pulled the plug on W&L at the end of 2018.) I'm not addicted to social media, and I don't enjoy it that much, but I'm addicted to feedback and affirmation. I read the comments and check the likes and retweets a couple of times a day. It's like a dopamine drip in my pocket.

2×/year. My father is dying. Nothing imminent, but he's eighty-eight, which, generally speaking, means the end is nearer than farther. The last five years I've seen him (at most) twice a year. I wallpaper over this in my mind, as I actively make his life more comfortable and I call him every Sunday. However, any honest appraisal yields a coarse truth . . . I'm not the son I want to be.

400. For the past fifteen years, I have taught, on average, four hundred students a year. I like the kids; they (mostly) like me and feel as if I am adding value. A bunch reach out to me on a regular basis and express gratitude and admiration, which makes me feel relevant.

3, 4, and 2. I've started nine companies: three were wins, four were failures, and two were somewhere in between. I don't believe any culture or country, other than the United States, would have given me this many chances.

Benchmarks, metrics, and milestones range from the meaningless to the profound. Accountability and insight are the by-products of math. Numbers yield insights about markets, how value is created, and how we want to live our lives. A review of the metrics in your life is a healthy exercise. In sum, I need to visit my dad.

Know the Ends vs. the Means

WHEN I was a freshman at UCLA, David Carey was a senior. We were in the same fraternity and knew each other, but we weren't friends, as we couldn't have been more different. David was in a serious relationship with a girl named Laurie and was the publisher of our school newspaper, the *Daily Bruin*. He wore big glasses and looked forty. I was too immature to be in a relationship, had a ponytail, smoked a lot of pot, and rowed crew. Thirty years later, David is married to Laurie, oversees Hearst's magazine business, has big glasses, and looks forty. I still smoke pot, but I am an entirely different person. David has changed less than any person I've ever known, in a good way.

In my twenties, I knew of David's professional progress, as conversation among friends from college inevitably turns to "Who's killing it?" David was always on that list. He was one of the youngest publishers in the business (*SmartMoney*— remember them?). David then landed big jobs at Condé Nast, including publisher of *The New Yorker*, while still in his thirties. David would regularly reach out and invite me to have lunch with him at Condé Nast, where we'd venture to the Frank Gehry–designed cafeteria and eat sushi among impossibly stylish young people whose parents were putting them through fashion. Anna Wintour would be in the corner booth with S. I. Newhouse Jr. At the time I was starting tech firms in San Francisco and was surrounded by people who lit up a room by leaving it. But I'd come to New York, where we'd have lunch next to the Prada-wearing devil. It felt more than relevant; it felt fabulous. In exchange, when my VCs would start harping about building a brand, I'd overpay for pages in *The New Yorker* and *InStyle*. One day, while eating in that cafeteria, I decided to move to New York.

After David's stint at Condé Nast, he'd invite me to lunch on the fifty-fifth floor of Hearst Tower in a private dining room for two, where a suited waiter would bring us some puff pastry the company was known for. By this time, I was teaching at NYU and had nothing to offer David professionally. But

I'd become a friend, and David lived by a code that included reaching out to friends on a regular basis. We now have almost no professional overlap. I wrote an article for *Esquire* (his idea), but we don't work together. Despite this, we've become closer. Mostly due to a common shared blessing we didn't recognize at eighteen or twenty-two, but one that has gained purchase in our minds as we've aged. Both of us came from middle-class families in Los Angeles. The generosity of California taxpayers and the vision of the Regents of the University of California lifted us up and gave us a shot at relevance and rewarding lives.

In 2018, David announced he was stepping down from his position as president of Hearst Magazines. At our most recent lunch, he shared his plans to step down. It didn't make any sense to me, as David is still relatively young, and well thought of at Hearst—a great firm that's good to its people. I suggested he stay, as he was "rounding third" and should enjoy the seat for a few more years. For the first time, I sensed unchecked emotion from David (he's a rock). He replied, "I want to help young people, and I'm sick of firing my friends."

It's easy to be admirable when you're an executive in a

sector growing 50 percent a year. To leave the print industry with friends and reputation intact is to win the Boston Marathon sporting a 104-degree fever.

David is a role model for me. Not because of his professional success; I know a lot of very successful people. But because David never lost the script . . . as I and many, or most, ambitious people have at some point in our lives. Professional success is the means, not the end. The end is economic security for your family and, more important, meaningful relationships with family and friends. David has been married to Laurie for over three decades, has four impressive adult children who are always around (always) and clearly adore their father. He has friends who admire him and feel admired by him.

We ended up in similar places professionally (I'm being generous to me). My ascent was fueled by the University of California, hard work, and a tolerance for risk. David's rise was a function of the University of California, hard work, and character.

Learn from Rejection

IN HIGH school, I ran for sophomore, junior, and senior class president. I lost all three times. Based on this track record, it was obvious I should run for student body president. I did, and I (wait for it) lost. I was also cut from the baseball and basketball teams. I remember my mom and I going to Junior's Deli on Sepulveda to celebrate my admittance to UCLA after initially being rejected.

Arriving on campus, I rushed five different fraternities and got admitted to one, as they were looking to fill a room in the house with someone who'd help pay the dues. When I graduated, I interviewed at twenty-two firms and got one offer, from Morgan Stanley.

I applied to several MBA programs and was rejected by Stanford, Indiana, Wharton, Duke, UT Austin, and Kellogg. I was admitted by UCLA and Berkeley Haas with the same narrative I pitched to UCLA the first time: "I'm an unremark-able kid, but I'm your [California's] unremarkable kid."

In business school, I ran for class president, and lost. Since graduating from business school, I have started nine businesses. Most have failed.

Serendipity Is a Function of Courage

I enjoy alcohol, but it's also served a useful evolutionary purpose, as it's dramatically increased my pool of potential mates. In social situations, "alcamahol" has been Kevlar against rejection. I'm a better version of myself after a couple of drinks:

funnier, more affectionate, confident, engaged, nicer . . . better. (Can't wait for the judge-mail on this one.) I remember being at the pool at the Raleigh Hotel in Miami Beach and seeing a woman I was incredibly drawn to. I committed myself to speaking to her before I left, and immediately (not proud of this) ordered a drink. Asking a VC for money is nothing compared to approaching a woman midday in a beach chair, sitting with another woman and a guy, and opening. I tell my students that nothing wonderful, I'm talking really fantastic, will happen without taking a risk and subjecting yourself to rejection. Serendipity is a function of courage.

My willingness to endure rejection from universities, peers, investors, and women has been hugely rewarding. Knowing what you want is a blessing, and fear of rejection is a bigger obstacle than lack of talent or the market. Train yourself to take some sort of risk (ask for a raise, introduce yourself around at a party) every day and get comfortable grasping beyond your reach.

My oldest son's middle name is Raleigh.

If You're Not an Employee, Employ Yourself

---

employee

/em'ploiē/

A person hired to provide services to a company on a regular basis in exchange for compensation.

I'm now an employee of Gartner, the firm that acquired L2. It's been less painful, though still painful, than expected, as the people are smart and nice. The last time I was an employee was twenty-five years ago at Morgan Stanley, my first job after UCLA. I had dozens of part-time jobs, but nothing with health benefits or the expectation of being an agent of the firm. Being an employee, and the wage-for-labor compact, is key to capitalism and something Americans are good at. Most Americans, that is.

The skills and attributes necessary to be an entrepreneur

are celebrated in the media every day—vision, risk-taking, grit. But few mention the skills needed to be a good employee. I possess almost none of them. People assume that because I'm an entrepreneur, I have extraordinary talents too big for a company. The truth about 90-plus percent of entrepreneurs is that we start companies not because we're so skilled, but because we don't have the skills to be an effective employee. On a risk-adjusted basis, being an employee for a good or great firm is more rewarding than being an entrepreneur. Again, something not discussed in a media obsessed with "innovators."

Some of those attributes:

1. **Being a grown-up.** Yeah, it sucks to be a grown-up and have to do things you may not want to do or that may not make sense. Commuting to and from work at the exact apex of traffic congestion and going to meetings that have no relevance to your job make no sense. But they're paying you and hopefully covering the cost to have that mole removed. Being an adult is about recognizing that it's not all about you.

   Working for yourself, everything you do is mostly for you. At the time, your actions make sense, as you're in charge.

Yesterday, we came into the office to find corporate calendars on our desks with inspirational quotes for each month. In January, we're to "Discover, Learn & Grow." Good to know. I believe posting inspirational quotes in the workplace qualifies as employee abuse. Writing about it helps.

2. **Civility.** Because I'm an entrepreneur and usually the guy in charge, people have romanticized my candor as vision and leadership. However, this mix of anger, honesty, and feedback wouldn't fly in an employee, since there's a difference between being right and being effective. Employees must navigate the two and realize they are part of a team, and they need to be supportive of one another. Show me an asshole in a small- to medium-size firm—that's usually the guy or gal who runs the place. As a firm gets bigger, the top person can't be a jerk, as this "radical candor" doesn't scale well. Small firms thrive on six to twelve A players working their asses off who are intolerably impatient. Big firms scale with hundreds or thousands of well-mannered B+ players.

3. **Being secure with yourself.** Working for other people means living in the unknown. You often find yourself unable to interpret verbal or nonverbal cues, or your review, for that

matter. You're not sure what the people who can shape your economic well-being have planned, or not planned, for you. Right out of college, I was deeply insecure (now I'm just insecure), and every time people went into a conference room I assumed they were talking about me. It wasn't vision but insecurity that led me to entrepreneurship.

Now, as an employee of Gartner, I endure a fraction of the BS most employees do, and am more Zen about it. I don't know if they're scared of me, have no idea what to do with me, or just don't give a damn . . . but they generally leave me alone and are supportive. It's strange being an employee, with no direct reports in the company you founded . . . discovering via email, like everyone else, what the firm has planned. I'm floating in space a bit. A nice shiny suit, people impressed, a nice view (i.e., success), but not tethered to the mother ship anymore. The insecurity is setting in again. *Do I add value? What am I doing here? Do they like me?*

Namath

The most rewarding part of my job is when young people who trust me seek counsel from me about their next move or other work matters. At this age, some of the kids, as I call them, become your adult kids, and you become concerned about their well-being. It's rewarding, as it scratches a maternal/paternal itch we have as we get older.

I'm Joe Namath dropping in on a Jets practice. Everyone is respectful of what I've built and wants to meet or speak to me. However, I'm worried I'll soon be Drunk Joe Namath, where everyone is trying to figure out the polite (and least awkward) way of telling me to leave the building. It's coming. Until then, I'm in their employ.

Be a Role Model

IN JUNIOR high, I was invisible.

In second grade, I was the only son in a nuclear family where Dad was a vice president for International Telegraph and Telegram (ITT) and Mom was a secretary. We lived in a house in Laguna Niguel overlooking the Pacific. By eighth grade, I was the son of a single mother (still a secretary), living in a condo in Westwood. In third grade, Debbie Brubaker and I were sent to the fifth grade for math and English. By the eighth grade, I was failing calculus, and my teacher suggested I be downgraded to Algebra II.

In fourth grade, I made the all-star baseball team as a pitcher and shortstop. By eighth grade, a growth spurt unaccompanied by weight gain blessed me with the height of a thirteen-year-old and the coordination and strength of a nine-year-old. I was now at a bigger, integrated school. We had a kid who, in the eighth grade, could dunk. My two best friends' parents pulled them from Emerson, deciding an integrated school wasn't right for their kids, and sent them to private schools.

I was maturing from remarkable to remarkably unremarkable. Not excelling at anything, few friends, no real sense of self. Invisible.

My mom's boyfriend, Randy, lived in Reno and owned a restaurant supplies company. He was rich, or seemed rich. More than that, he was generous and engaged in the well-being of his girlfriend's son. Randy would spend every other weekend with us. I was always welcome on the trips they took, and he bought me my first nice skateboard, a Bahne. Randy paid the mortgage on our condo in Westwood, which my mom, as a secretary, could not have afforded. He made our lives tangibly better. Randy was also married, with a school-age son of his own, but that's another story.

One Sunday evening, as he was packing to leave, I asked Randy about stocks. I had heard Jerry Dunphy, the local news anchor, reference the stock market on TV. As I watched Randy fold sweaters and place awesome toiletries in his leather Dopp kit (English Leather, Barbasol, and Skin Bracer . . . by Mennen), he gave me an overview of the markets. When the taxi honked, I carried his bag down. Randy stopped at the dining room table, took out his wallet, placed two crisp $100 bills on the table, and said, "Go buy some stock at one of those fancy brokers in the Village." I asked how I would do that. "You're bright enough to figure it out, and if you don't by the time I'm back, I want my money back." I had never seen a hundred-dollar bill before.

I placed them under a volume of my *Encyclopedia Britannica,* and the next day after school I marched down to the corner of Westwood and Wilshire and into the office of Merrill Lynch, Pierce, Fenner & Smith. I sat in the reception area, and . . . I was invisible. They weren't unfriendly or mean—I was just invisible. I began to feel self-conscious, despite being invisible. I left and walked across the street into the offices of Dean Witter Reynolds. A woman with big gold jewelry asked if she could help me, and I told her I was there to buy stock. She paused. I became self-conscious again and blurted, "I have two hundred dollars," and took the crisp bills out of an envelope I had put them in that morning. She jumped up, gave me a clear-window envelope, and told me to wait a minute. Sitting, I re-arranged the bills in my new envelope so I could see Ben

Franklin's hair and ear through the cellophane. A young man with curly hair approached me, asked my name, and introduced himself.

"I'm Cy Cordner.* Welcome to Dean Witter."

Cy took me to his office and gave me a thirty-minute lesson in the markets. The ratio of buyers to sellers determined price movements. Each share represented a small piece of ownership. You could buy stocks in companies whose products you liked or admired. Amateurs act on emotion, pros on numbers. We decided to invest my bounty in thirteen shares of Columbia Pictures, ticker CPS, at $15 ⅜.

Each weekday for the next two years, at lunch, I'd go to the phone booth on the main field with two dimes and call Cy to discuss my portfolio. Sometimes after school, I'd walk to his office to get the update in person (see above: few friends). He'd type in the ticker and tell me what CPS had done that day and speculate why the stock had moved: "The markets were down today." "It looks like *Close Encounters of the Third Kind* is a hit." "*Casey's Shadow* is a bomb." Cy also took the time to call my

---

* This is a pseudonym.

mom. Not to pitch her for business (we had no money), but to let her know what we discussed in the calls and say nice things about me.

The story would be more fun if I'd ended up a billionaire hedge fund manager. I'm not. But I know more about the markets than most marketing professors, and it's served me well. Really well even. More important, at thirteen, I was visible. Visible and worthy of an impressive man's time, every day. Randy and Cy instilled in me that remarkable men can become irrationally passionate about the well-being of a child . . . who isn't theirs. After heading to high school, I lost touch with Cy and, several years later, sold the stock to pay for a road trip to Ensenada with my UCLA friends.

Pay It Back

In my forties, I became blessed with greater self-awareness. Aware of my strengths, weaknesses, blessings, and what makes me happy. Problem is, I also became more aware of my deficits— where I had taken more than given. Friends who invested more in the relationship than me. Partners/girlfriends who had been more committed and generous. Even California taxpayers, paying for my education at UCLA, and me reciprocating with striking underachievement—a 2.27 GPA (no joke). Taking, always taking.

I've been trying to fix that, and decided to track down Cy ten years ago to say thanks. Googled him every which way, even called Dean Witter (now Morgan Stanley), but no luck. Chances are he's keeping a low profile, or maybe he's totally off the grid. I tell the story to my class when discussing mentors and how many strangers' acts of kindness have had an impact on my life and prosperity. For the last decade, I have challenged

them (offering a $5,000 bounty) to find Cy, as I know they'll come up empty-handed.

"We Found Cy Cordner"

In my spring 2018 Brand Strategy class, the day after issuing the challenge to the 170 kids, I received not one, not two, but three emails with the same subject line: "We found Cy Cordner." The three budding Magnum P.I.s had found Cy's nephew on Facebook, reached out to him, and gotten his phone number. (Important to highlight one of the millions of good things that happen on the social platform, as I've been throwing a lot of shade at Facebook recently.) I called Cy later that week and we spoke for an hour. Our lives charted eerily similar paths: UCLA, financial services (both of us Morgan Stanley, via Dean Witter for Cy), divorce, two kids, and then entrepreneurship. After his divorce, Cy wanted to be closer to his daughters and moved to Oregon, where he owns a retail store called Monaco that sells high-end furniture. He's hoping to retire next year.

After our first contact in forty years, I received the following email from Cy:

Cy Cordner <xxxxx@gmail.com>
Mar 27, 2018

Dear Professor Galloway {Scott},

It was an absolute pleasure speaking with you yesterday. Your life has traveled a remarkable path and in many cases parallel to my own life. When we completed our call I shared with my girlfriend much of the background of our conversation. She was equally amazed! Allow me to take a moment and distill my thoughts and feelings. Your perseverance and success reflect your upbringing and the love of your mom. Additionally, your character as a young boy who (as I) had an incredible thirst for knowledge is most apparent. I am proud that we met when you were so young and that I made a constructive impression on you. I AM VERY PROUD OF YOU!

I look forward to the prospect of meeting again. If you ever need anything, simply, contact me anytime.

Sincerely,
Cy Cordner

Forty years later, I'm thirteen again with a generous man who makes me feel less invisible.

Approaching his seventieth birthday, Cy is taking stock of his blessings, getting remarried, thinking of selling his business, and easing into retirement. At fifty-four, I'm also taking stock of my blessings, and trying to repair my deficits.

Love

The Ends

LOVE AND relationships are the ends—everything else is just the means. We, as a species, segment love. When we are young, we take in love—our parents', teachers', caregivers'. When we enter adulthood, we find transactional love; we love others in exchange for something in return—their love, security, or intimacy. Then there's complete love, surrendering to loving someone regardless of whether they love you back, or whether you get anything in return, for that matter. No conditions, no exchange, just a decision to love this person and focus solely on their well-being.

Love received is comforting, love reciprocated is rewarding, and love given completely is eternal. You are immortal. Our role, our job as agents of the species, is to love someone unconditionally. It's the secret sauce cementing the survival of *Homo sapiens*. And to ensure we continue to enlist in this act, nature made it the most rewarding. To love someone completely is the ultimate accomplishment. It tells the universe you matter, you are an agent of survival, evolution, and life. You are still just a blink of an eye, but the blink matters.

The Most Important Decision

The key decision you'll make in life is who you have kids with. Who you marry is meaningful; who you have kids with is profound. (Note: I don't believe you need to be married to have a wonderful life.) Raising kids with someone who is kind and competent and who you enjoy being with is a series of joyous moments smothered in comfort and reward. Raising kids with someone you don't like, or who isn't competent, is moments of joy smothered in anxiety and disappointment.

Building a life with someone who loves you, and who you love, near guarantees a life of reward interrupted by moments of pure joy. Sharing your life with someone who's unstable or has contempt for you is never being able to catch your breath long enough to relax and enjoy your blessings.

Someone Who Likes You

How do you go about finding such a person? Young people need to try to override the emotion of scarcity. Let me explain. Key to evolution is trying to punch above your weight class and mix your DNA with someone who has better DNA—natural selection. People rejecting your overtures is a relatively accurate indicator that you are in fact punching too high. You will, on a balanced scorecard, likely end up with someone in your weight class in terms of character, success, looks, and pedigree. Rejection is an immediate and credible message that the object of your affections has better DNA than you, and knows it. Problem is, you begin associating rejection with better DNA to a fault. I'm not suggesting people shouldn't reach beyond their weight class (a key attribute for success) and not ask out the tall guy with the great hair. But young people stand to benefit from one simple thing:

Like someone who likes you.

Someone who thinks you're great is a feature . . . not a bug. I've found that most young people don't end up with someone until there has been some form of rejection from the other . . . which is interpreted as a signal of superior DNA. Yes, punch above your weight class . . . but don't fall into the trap of believing someone is better because they're not that into you. And if someone thinks you're the bomb, it doesn't mean they're below your weight class or somehow not worthy.

My dog, Zoe, picks the person who loves her the most. She's the Oprah of relationships. Zoe, and all of us, reach contentment when we recognize a shortcut to happiness: finding someone who chooses you over everything, and everyone, else.

1 + 1 > 2

I HAVE a friend, a successful hedge fund manager, who moved to Cascais, a small town outside Lisbon, Portugal. He wanted to reset his life—focus more on family and take advantage of Portugal's quality of life. He stays with me when he's in town, which I enjoy, as NYU faculty housing in winter is a bit lonely—depressing, even (hold me). Despite being a master of the universe, he has strong nurturing instincts and takes care of people around him naturally. Last night I came home, and he announced that we were going to Soho House for dinner.

We ran into two friends, one recently engaged and the other recently divorced. We congratulated the younger friend on his upcoming nuptials and then got on with the important work of understanding every detail of being single at our age.

Tindering

What became clear was that, while it has its moments, being single is a lot of work. The prepping, pruning, preening, planning, Tindering, texting, courting, rejecting, Coachella-ing, gaming, and being rejected are exhausting. Being good at being single either means you're one of the 1 percent who don't live in the real world and everything just sort of comes to you (I know a few of these people and hate them), or—like any job—you have to work at it.

Studies show that marriage is advantageous economically. Having a partnership, sharing expenses and responsibilities, being able to focus on your careers, and utilizing the wisdom of crowds (couples) generally leads to better decisions ("No, we're not buying a boat"). There is a streamlining of choices, which lets you allocate your attention capital to things that grow, instead of decline, in value (your career vs. your attractiveness to others or being seen at the right places).

Once married, your household worth grows at an average of 14 percent a year. Married couples, by their fifties, on average have 3x the assets of their single peers. The key? Taking the whole "till death do us part" thing seriously, as divorce seriously eats into the 3x. From an evolutionary perspective, monogamous relationships improve survival odds for offspring, benefiting our species overall.

Try to Be a Partner

Marriage dates back to ancient societies. Our ancestors needed a safe environment in which to have children and a way to handle property rights. Marriages based on love didn't become popular until the Romantic era. The engagement ring, a custom dating back to ancient Rome, is a circle symbolizing eternity and everlasting union. It was once believed that a vein or nerve ran directly from the "ring finger" of the left hand to the heart.

I'm good at marriage; done it twice. One marriage was good, the other great. My first marriage ended not because it was bad, but because I wanted to be single. But that's another story.

Here is the advice on marriage I offer when asked to give a toast at a wedding. It's through a male lens (can't help that).

Don't keep score. It's human nature to inflate your own contribution to the relationship and minimize your partner's. Couples who are always taking notes on who's done what for whom waste energy, and ultimately both feel as if they're in the loss column. Decide if the relationship as a whole gives you joy and comfort, and if it does (and it better, at this point), then commit to always being on the positive side of the ledger—aim to be generous and do as much as you can for your partner, as often as possible.

Be willing to wipe the slate clean if and when your partner messes up, as she or he will. Studies show that forgiveness is a key attribute to sustainable, happy relationships. One of the main components of our success as a nation is that we give people a second chance. It's no different in relationships—achieving real love and a sense of partnership will likely involve forgiveness that, at the time, feels unfair and even embarrassing.

As we get older, we get more reward from giving. Keeping score creates a dynamic where you never give in to the real joy in life . . . doing something for someone because you love them and choose their happiness over everything else, full stop. Caregivers are the most important contributors to the species and are rewarded with longer lives. Marriage is a promise to give care, every day.

Don't ever let your wife be cold or hungry. I mean . . . ever. In retrospect, most of the really awful fights I've had with partners have been because we managed to skip lunch. Invest in dual-zone climate control cars, and when you sit down at a restaurant, before you do anything, ensure you are not dining with Satan—a draft of cold air. Try to never leave the house without energy bars and one of those oversized cashmere scarves that can double as a blanket. You're welcome.

Express affection and desire as often as possible. Affection, touch, and sex reinforce that your relationship is singular. That this person, when all else is stripped away, is who you want. We are animals, and affection and sex are where you can be most who you really are. People who don't feel desired are more likely to feel insecure, and to like themselves less around you, which can metastasize into the cancers of relationships: indifference and contempt.

In my experience, the most rewarding things in life are family and professional achievement. Without someone to share these things with, you've seen a ghost—it sort of happened, but not really. However, with the right partner, these things feel real, you feel more connected to the species, and all "this" begins to register meaning.

"I do" means "I will . . . care for, shelter, nourish, and want you."

Keep Your Kids Close

WHEN MY oldest was two, he'd wake up at dawn, gather some of his most precious possessions (Matchbox cars), put them in a wicker basket, and head to our room. He would stand at the door and extend the basket, a nonverbal offering of sorts, in exchange for us letting him into bed with us. We would refuse and take him back to his bed. This cycle would repeat every fifteen minutes for the next two hours until we all got up. Several mornings we found him asleep just outside our door, wanting to come in but too afraid of being rejected.

There are few things about parenting I regret more than turning away our oldest from joining us in sleep.

Our intentions were good. Western research on co-sleeping emphasizes the importance of kids developing coping systems and confidence from sleeping on their own. Also it's important that parents nourish their own relationship and intimacy. But there's no one-size-fits-all here, and most cultures lean on the side of a pack approach to sleep. (Note: I'm talking about parents co-sleeping with young children, as there are safety risks associated with co-sleeping with infants.) It takes a few books on raising kids to realize one thing: nobody has an algorithm for successful parenting.

I counsel new parents to do what feels right for them and to trust their instincts. Our instinct, and what we've done the last several years, is to ensure that everyone starts in their own bed (though our dog sleeps at the foot of the bed of our youngest), and see how things play out the rest of the night. Some nights everyone wakes up where they started; most nights there are three or four in our bed. Occasionally I exit the crowded parking lot and enjoy some solo slumber in the recently vacated bed of my oldest.

In the United States, parents are closeted about the amount of co-sleeping that takes place. We've been inculcated in the bullshit notion that it's unnatural. There are few things that feel more natural. The Japanese are big on co-sleeping, referring to the practice as "the river": mom and dad as the banks, the child in between as the water.

The waters in our bed are serene rivers that storm unexpectedly, delivering kicks to the face and errant questions ("Dad, is it time to get up?" "No, go back to sleep."). My youngest is most comfortable sleeping perpendicular across my throat like a 35-pound bow tie. This is strangely relaxing for me, and I nod off. Or it could be mild asphyxiation that renders me unconscious. My oldest likes to have one foot touching his mom or dad, at all times. He will sit up every ninety minutes and just look around the room, then go back to sleep.

My dad's biggest fear, as a child of the Depression, is that he'll die broke (he's fine). My biggest fear is that my selfish tendencies translate to a lack of investment in relationships, and I'll die alone. One place I've invested, early and often, is in my boys. I'm banking on the small investments made several times a week in the middle of the night paying off. Less space in bed, errant bruises, and generally less sleep are deposits compounding toward one goal: that they will remember their parents chose them over anything else.

We come into and leave this world alone and vulnerable, wanting the touch of people we know love us so we can sleep in peace. I trust that these investments will make it instinctual for our boys, when their mom and dad are old and vulnerable, to lie with and comfort us . . . so we can sleep in peace.

I ♥ U

WE HAVE friends, a couple, who lost an extended family member to ALS. Soon after, they took stock of their blessings and asked each other, "What could we do to better seize the moments that are our life?" The husband is an adventurer and proposed that, with their three kids, they circumnavigate the globe in a high-tech catamaran. This would be insane if they weren't both uber-competent people whom others trust with their lives and livelihoods (she's a doc, he's a CEO). Even so, cruising around on the open ocean supported by two giant boogie boards feels a tad crazy.

They did a test run, a week at sea, which I followed closely on Instagram. The night watches, rough seas, engine trouble . . . all of it. I didn't get it. This seemed more like punishment than taking life by the horns. And then, in one image, it became clear. The husband's joy was evident, even in 2D. To be with his family, applying their skills, strength, and wits to embrace and conquer nature made him glow. No filter. Partners who can take what they've built together and throw the full force of that at each other's happiness are likely the root of our prosperity as a species. The most rewarding things in life aren't accoutrements or our technological progress (Cartier or Boeing) but things that have been baked into us over millions of years to augment the species.

As my first marriage was crumbling, part of my penance was going to couples therapy. To my surprise, I enjoyed it. Our therapist was a smart, caring man who seemed generally interested in my favorite topic . . . me. I asked my therapist, Boris (real name), for his definition of love. Boris felt love was a willingness to take the life you've built for yourself and tear it up for the other person. If you're wondering what happened, let's just say that, at thirty-three, I didn't let my spouse change the radio station in our car . . . much less reconfigure my life. So fucking selfish.

By this measure, I had never really loved anybody until I had kids. Instinctively and proactively, we suspend our lives and shape them around our kids. It took a while for me (see above: selfish). Babies are awful. But slowly instinct kicked in, and weekends are now soccer matches, birthday parties, and *Despicable Me 3*. Brunch with friends, TV, and sleeping in were great, but there's a comfort in having the same answer to most of life's questions: whatever is best for the kids. People without kids bask in the same light when they're kind and caring to others.

Montezuma's Revenge

I'M HAVING trouble connecting with my youngest son—he's six. My oldest, nine, spoils me, as we love to watch and play soccer together, and he, for some reason, thinks I'm the bomb. My youngest, not so much. However, recently I discovered he enjoys roller coasters. I get motion sick in elevators but willingly endure terror and nausea on Montezuma's Revenge, a ride at Knott's Berry Farm. He laughs uncontrollably the entire ride and, at the end, will ask, "Wasn't that great?" I lie, "Yes . . . great . . ." In that moment we're closer.

The other night we were with the boys at a family restaurant where there was a talent show. They had open-mic karaoke, and my older son, much to my horror, volunteered. He requested the Justin Bieber song "Sorry." The words on the screen came too fast, and he froze. I instinctively leapt to his side and began whispering the words in his ear to get him back on track.

There are few things I hate more than Justin Bieber or karaoke. But the things you hate become just inconveniences in the presence of people you love. Catamarans, roller coasters, and karaoke. Different ways of saying the same thing: *My life is yours, and I love you.*

Valentine's Day

VALENTINE'S DAY has morphed into a celebration of romantic love, but according to Wikipedia, it honors two early saints named Valentinus. One of these men, while jailed for performing weddings for soldiers, restored the sight of the blind daughter of the judge who had imprisoned him. Before his execution, he wrote the girl a letter and signed it "Your Valentine."

CrossFit

You've heard the joke: "How do you know someone does Cross-Fit? They tell you."

So, I do CrossFit. Working out, for me, pre-forty, was so I could be more attractive and feel better about myself, as I suffer from body dysmorphic disorder. Post-forty, I exercise to get my head right (as an antidepressant) and to cling to life—to feel less old. There's a decent amount of research indicating that exercise is the only real youth serum. I'm usually the oldest guy in the class by two decades, which should be cool. But it isn't.

You see, they treat me like Mick Jagger—so old, they find me inspiring. I walk into the box (what CrossFit calls gyms, for some reason), and the earnest comments begin ("It's so great you're here!"). Yeah, fuck you.

Often, the workout is a race against the clock, and I'll still be working through my box jumps, burpees, and various forms of torture when others begin checking their phones and fist-bumping one another, already finished. Then something awful

happens. They spot me (still) making the movements of a fish that's been on a hard surface for too long, flopping every once in a while and gasping. They'll surround me, no joke, start clapping, and say shit like . . . "You got this, Scott!" It's awful.

Anyway, the coach at my NYC box is a kid named Sean. He's twenty-three, looks fifteen, has black curly hair, wears neon red basketball shorts and a hoodie, and takes himself, and CrossFit, very seriously. A month ago I got to class ten minutes late, and he told me in front of the class—of other twentysomethings—"If you're late next time, I'm not going to let you into class." (Ironic, given my personal late policy; see page 48.)

Note: If it sounds as if I am guilty of asking people to "do as I say, not as I do," then (again) trust your instincts.

I was twenty minutes late recently for a live TV segment on CNBC's *Squawk Box*, and . . . they switched segments around. But not Sean—he'd had enough. Probably a good thing. I recognize I need to be reminded I'm not that important—home is a volcano of reminders.

Tell People You Love Them

Ten minutes into class, we find ourselves on the floor stretching, and my mind begins to focus on the horror that awaits me
in the remainder of the hour. Wednesday, Valentine's Day, I
went to the 7:30 p.m. class, and five minutes into the stretching, the very serious Sean heard a distinct ringtone on his
phone. An emergency? He retreated to the corner, near where
I was stretching (i.e., lying on my back occasionally moving a
limb to one side). Sean answered the phone:

"Hi, Grandpa, I'm at work, can I call you back?"

However, Grandpa was having none of it. He ignored the
request and kept Sean on the phone. Every thirty seconds over
the next three minutes (I timed it, as I was bored—see above:
stretching), Sean would respond with the same five words: "I
love you, too, Grandpa." Six times.

I wondered what Grandpa was saying to Sean. Was he con-
soling him, because Sean didn't have anybody to spend Valentine's with? Maybe he was telling Sean about his grandma or
his mother, or maybe just using the holiday as an excuse to tell

Sean, repeatedly, how wonderful he is. What was clear is that, six times, he told his grandson, "I love you."

Perspective

Old people get up close and personal with death as their friends and spouses begin departing, which heaps perspective on them. Marketers hate old people because of this perspective. They begin spending their time and money on things like healthcare, loved ones, and college funds for their grandkids instead of vintage sneakers, iPhones, and Keurig pods. In sum, they become fearful and remarkably less stupid . . . refusing to spend money on high-margin products that young people hope will make them feel more attractive or powerful.

We invest so much in our kids. Sitting on the sidelines as your nine-year-old goalie son reaches in vain for eleven shots that find the net behind him, or attempting to digest the food at a water park. The payoff? Several decades later, you can in terrupt your kid's kid at work, ignore their requests to call you back, and every thirty seconds tell him you love him, pause, and hear your grandson tell you he loves you, too. Wash, rinse, repeat . . . six times.

I have a love/hate relationship with CrossFit. However, I've decided I like Sean.

Taking Affection Back

In a piece on Medium, Mark Greene argues that affection has been taken away from males—and that's hurting us all. I believe him. As boys, we're trained that affection is either a means of progressing to sex or a signal of homosexuality—which was, when and where I grew up, a bad thing. Because of these associations—unwelcome sexual motive or homoeroticism—our touch is not trusted, so most males are robbed of affection. It's lost from our arsenal of expressions to signal friendship, fondness, or love.

Touch is truly fundamental to human communication, bonding, and health . . . [T]ouch activates the brain's orbitofrontal cortex, which is linked to feelings of reward and compassion . . . [T]ouch signals safety and trust, it soothes.

—Dacher Keltner, professor of psychology, UC Berkeley

As I get older, I've made a conscious effort to take affection back, especially as it relates to my boys. It bonds us, and I'm fairly certain it will add confidence to their lives and years to mine.

Kissing

One of my closest friends, Lee, comes from an Italian family. I hung out with him and his dad one day. The thing I remember most is when his father showed up. He walked into the apartment, and he and Lee Jr. kissed . . . on the lips, as if they were shaking hands. I had never seen two grown men kiss before. Twenty years later, my other touchstone for Italian culture, *The Sopranos*, confirmed this is common practice. I remember, after the initial shock, thinking it was nice.

I kiss my boys, a lot. The act itself is nice, but the real reward is the respect my boys have for the moment. They can be watching TV, fighting, complaining (they complain a shit-ton), but when I signal the kiss (I lean in and pucker), they stop everything, angle their chin upward, and kiss me on the lips . . .

and then go back to what they were doing. It's as if they know this has meaning—the other stuff can wait a few seconds.

Hold Hands

I never enjoyed holding hands until I had kids. The things we do for our kids—the soccer practices, the worry, the carpools, the bad movies, setting up remote controls, working to give them a better life than yours. In isolation, each of these things is okay—tolerable, but nothing anybody who doesn't have kids would ever do. Have you seen *The Emoji Movie*? However, the sum of these parts forms and checks an instinctive box. It gives you the sense you're serving a larger purpose—the whole evolution thing.

Few things encapsulate this reward and distill it into a single action more than holding your child's hand. Every kid's hand fits perfectly into his or her parent's. It's one of those moments when you feel that if you were to drop dead, it would be bad, but far less tragic than if you had not marked the universe with purpose and success. You're a parent, and your kid is holding your hand.

My oldest is holding my hand less, as he's ten and feeling his independence. At least he doesn't freak out and scream,

"Stop it!" like the fourteen-year-old girl I overheard on the soccer field tonight, whose mom had committed the crime against humanity of grabbing her teenage daughter's hand. My guess is, later the daughter felt bad.

My youngest, seven, still instinctively grabs my hand whenever we're walking outside, and it's magical. He's a barbarian at home, terrorizing us all. But out in the wild he's a bit intimidated and wants the security of touch from someone he knows will protect him. He goes for his mom's hand first. I'm runner-up . . . and that's okay.

I started registering the individuality of my parents at six or seven. Parents are like consumer brands in that, as kids, we remember only two or three key things about them, missing the nuance you only appreciate as you get older and realize people are complicated. My mom was smart, loved me, and was no-nonsense. My dad was intense and quiet around us as a family, but uber-charming and outgoing around strangers.

Hard to speculate what your kids will remember about you when they're older. I've inherited some of the anger and intensity of my father, which makes our home less light than it could be. But I'm committed to ensuring that some of my kids' associations with me are "always kissing us, always extending his hand."

If men who look like Burt Reynolds can kiss other men, so can I. I'm taking affection back.

Divorce

WE'VE BEEN reading words for several hundred years, listening to words for thousands, and learning from images for millions of years. We, as a species, are great with images. We can interpret/absorb an image fifty times faster than words, as we've had a lot more practice with visuals. Just as music is cemented into our being in the late teen years, the images of our early childhood become fixed into our gray matter.

When I was seven, we lived in a house near the beach in Laguna Niguel. My dad would come home early and we'd go body-surfing and see seals and porpoises just offshore. When there was a storm, in the morning we'd go to Newport Beach. From the end of the pier we'd look several hundred feet out and alert each other when millions of gallons, barreling toward shore, morphed into a blue-gray hemicylinder, eight, maybe ten feet high, and wait for the pier to shake as the rising sea floor thrust the cylinder up and the wave crashed down on the water.

One of four consecutive nights, beginning on the full and new moons in spring, my mom would wake me at midnight and, armed with flashlights, we'd go down to the beach and watch what looked like hot slices of metal dancing in the shallow surf. The grunion were running.

They weren't all images from the title sequence of *The O.C.* I remember seeing, on TV, a skinny guy wearing a ski mask on a hotel balcony interrupting awe-inspiring performances from Mark Spitz and Olga Korbut. The only reason it stuck is every time this guy came on screen, my parents stood in front of the TV, visibly uncomfortable.

When my father was going on a business trip, my mom and I would go with him to Orange County Airport. More than an airport, it felt like a restaurant where people pulled up, in the back, in commercial aircraft. There was a bar and wraparound balcony on the second floor that you could access via stairs from the street. No security. My dad would take me out on the balcony and cover my ears as aircraft engines screamed in anticipation of the pilot releasing the brakes. They would begin their 5,700-foot transformation from beached seals to soaring eagles.

He taught me the difference between a 727 and a DC-9 (three jets vs. two), and between the DC-10 and the L-1011 (the third jet is part of the fuselage vs. finding residence halfway up the tail). The backyard of this restaurant was dominated by two brands, Air California and Pacific Southwest Airlines. Pacific planes had a smile painted on the nose, grinning at us through the big windows.

My parents were living the American Dream. Two immigrants with eighth-grade educations, they applied hard work and talent to the greatest force of good in history: the US economy. We lived close to the beach. But they (mostly my dad) fucked up, and soon we were living in two houses, neither near the beach. After the divorce, my dad would pick me up after work every other Friday in his Gran Torino, from my mom's 800-square-foot apartment in Encino. I had to wait outside, sometimes for an hour, far from our apartment, as my mom didn't want to risk seeing my dad, or even his car—she hated him. I became skilled at identifying cars, from a distance, by the shape and luminosity of their headlights. AMC Pacers were easiest.

Any time I hear sound in the air, I still look up and, most of the time, can identify the plane and airline. Recently on a weekend in South Beach, my friends pretended to be impressed with my ability to distinguish the double-decker Airbus A380 headed to Munich (Lufthansa) vs. the one headed to Paris (Air France). Gazing upward and cataloging air traffic is an instinct for me—look up, identify an object, and think of when we were a family and lived near the beach.

Attach to People

AFFECTION EXCHANGE theory, introduced by Professor Kory Floyd, postulates that affection strengthens bonds, provides access to resources, and communicates your potential as a parent, increasing your pool of potential mates. I think it goes even deeper. I know a lot of people who, despite their good fortune, are wandering. Few meaningful relationships, an inability to find reward in their professional lives, too hard on themselves, etc. It's as if they're not grounded, never convinced of their worth . . . wandering.

When I look at my own success, it mostly boils down to two things: being born in America and having someone irrationally passionate about my well-being—my mom. Though she was raised in a household where there was little affection, my mom couldn't control herself with her son. For me, affection was the difference between *hoping* someone thought I was wonderful and worthy—and knowing someone did.

Every Wednesday night after Boy Scouts, my mom and I would go to dinner at Junior's Deli on Sepulveda Boulevard in Culver City. I would have the brisket dip, she the lox, eggs, and onions. We talked about our week—we didn't see each other much between weekends—only to be interrupted by different waitresses, who would comment on how much I had grown.

On the way out, we'd stop at the bakery and buy a quarter pound of halvah. As we stood in the parking lot waiting for the valet to retrieve our lime-green Opel Manta, my mom would grab my hand and, in an exaggerated fashion, swing it back and forth. She'd look at me, and I would return her gaze with an eye roll, at which point she would burst into joyous, uncontrollable laughter. She loved me so much . . .

Having a good person express how wonderful you are hundreds of times changes everything. College, professional success, an impressive mate—these were aspirations, not givens for a remarkably unremarkable kid in an upper-lower-middle-class household. My mom was forty-three, single, and making

$15,000 a year as a secretary. She was also a good person who made me feel connected and, while waiting for our Opel, gave me the confidence that I had value, that I was capable and deserving of all these things. Holding hands and laughing, I was tethered.

What Makes a Home

IN A capitalist society, we mark life by our purchases. The first big purchase is an engagement ring that De Beers has convinced young men to massively overspend on, as it is a "store of value" and generally fits a strange notion that we are marking our property with an item that reflects our level of manhood . . .

how economically successful we are. The second big purchase: the home. The National Association of Realtors has deftly engendered the notion that the American Dream is homeownership. Ask somebody who purchased a home in 2007 if their "dreams" came true.

Yale economist and Nobel Prize winner Robert Shiller argues that, when maintenance is accounted for, a house isn't a much better investment than any other asset class. Still, we see our first home purchase as a sign of our progress and trajectory as adults, and it is a form of forced savings. The government has bought into this (see above: National Association of Realtors), and the interest on your mortgage is tax deductible. The mortgage tax deduction is one of the costliest tax breaks in America. Another? Lower taxation on capital gains, versus ordinary income. These are both positioned as "American": homeownership and investing. They are simply transfers of wealth from the poor to the rich. Who owns homes and stocks? Wealthy old people. Who rents and doesn't have assets that qualify for capital gains treatment? The young and the poor.

A better proxy for your life isn't your first home, but your last. Where you draw your last breath is more meaningful, as it's a reflection of your success and, more important, the number of people who care about your well-being. Toward the end, you aren't adding much value, and people who look out for you are either exceptionally generous or reciprocating your love and support.

My mom's last home was in a seniors community in Las Vegas. When she moved, I told her to throw out her old furniture, and we decorated the whole place in Pottery Barn—I had advised Williams-Sonoma on their internet strategy in the nineties, and their CMO, Pat Connolly, gave me a discount. It wasn't having club chairs and chenille pillows that gave my mom joy, but that her son had bought them for her.

When my mom got very sick and had several surgeries, the hospital moved her to long-term care. When I walked into the facility, it reeked of urine, and there were people asleep in wheelchairs in the hall. I walked into my mom's room, which she shared with another woman. Her roommate was bedridden and had a TV attached to a metal arm six inches from her face. The TV was blinking on and off. She looked at me and asked if it was too loud. My mom was sitting upright on the edge of her bed waiting for me. She looked at me and said, "I don't want to be here." All the fucking fake relevance, semi-internet fame, money, and living large . . . and my ninety-pound mom was trapped in a place that reeked of urine.

I had failed.

I helped my mom pack her stuff and told the nurses I wanted to take her home. They said that would be "against doctor's orders" and that they would call security if necessary. I went outside and told the driver who'd brought me there that I would be bringing my mom out in a wheelchair, and that we needed to get her in the car and leave promptly. I went back into the facility, got a wheelchair, put my mom in it, placed her bag on her lap, and headed out. As we passed the nurses' desk, they looked calmly at us, and a large security guard positioned himself between my mom and me and the sliding exit doors. He didn't say anything, just stood there.

This is where it would make for a better story if I had told him to get out of my way or, in a Morgan Freeman voice, announced, "I'm taking my mother home." But that's not what happened. I froze and stood there, with my hands on the handles of my mom's wheelchair, her in a hospital gown holding a duffel bag with her stuff. We all stood there for what was likely ten seconds but felt like ten minutes. I think he felt sorry for us. He turned his gaze to the floor and walked away, and we left. My mom passed seven weeks later, at home.

My dad and his wife recently moved into what will likely be their last home, as they are both eighty-eight. My sister, my dad's wife's children, and I pulled together to make the move easier and ensure it's a nice place. My dad told me this will be the first time he can truly relax, as he won't need to garden or take care of the house. It's a great place in a university town, with movie nights, on-call medical professionals, and a pool he can swim in, and we're arranging for a trainer so he can maintain his lifelong fitness routine.

Your first house signals the meaningful—your future and possibility. Your last home signals the profound—the people who love you.

How to Deal with the End of a Life

THE DAY after I spoke at a conference hosted by an internet giant, I got four messages on LinkedIn: three from people saying nice things about the talk and looking to connect, and one that rattled me. A twenty-six-year-old total stranger was asking me for advice. The message is below (I've changed her name and some details for anonymity).

Subject: Inquiry for Life Advice

Hi Professor Galloway,

I am reaching out because I trust your opinion and would love your advice.

I am 26 and have been building a career in digital marketing at a consumer products company in X. It has been a great opportunity to work with a passionate team on many data sets to solve uncommon creative problems and inform product development.

In January my dad was diagnosed with late-stage pancreatic cancer, and I have made the decision to move back home to be with him and my mom. I have been planning on continuing to work . . . but have this nagging feeling that it's not worth it, and the extra money is not as valuable as full days with my family during this time. Still I am worried that halting my learning right now will hinder my career in the long run.

I wish my dad was able to help me answer this question with a clear head and from an unbiased place. I would love your opinion on this as a second-best option!

Dear X,

I'm sorry about your dad. First, some fine print. I have no real credentials nor empirical data around providing comfort to sick parents. These are very personal decisions. What I can tell you is what I did when my mom was sick and what I learned. It's key to point out, however, that I was in a different stage in my career. I was 39 and had established some professional stature and economic security, which at 26 you likely don't have. There's no user manual around this stuff. A lot of it boils down to your relationship with your parent, logistics, and resources. So, with that:

My mom was diagnosed with metastatic stomach cancer and was given three months to live. She asked me if I could help her die at home, and I agreed. I moved in with her, at a retirement community in Summerlin, Nevada, so we could spend time together and make her exit more dignified. She passed seven months later at home. Where you die, and who is around you at the end, is a strong signal of your success or failure in life.

Learning: I believe it doesn't matter how nice your home is; if at your exit you're surrounded by strangers under bright lights, it's a disappointment. Granted this isn't an option for many people, but if you die at home, surrounded by people who love you, you are a success. It's a sign that you forged meaningful relationships and that you were generous with people. My mom had no education, was divorced, and worked as a secretary. She drew her last breath at home, comfortable and surrounded by people who loved her immensely. If you and your family can arrange for your father to die at home, you are doing something loving and kind for your dad.

Learning: Give care to the caregivers. My mom's four sisters and best friend each spent 3–4 weeks living with us helping to care for her. This was key, as there were things I couldn't help with. One way I was able to add value was to help make their stay more enjoyable. One of my aunts just loved to talk—I don't. I speak for a living, but when I'm home I want to hear my kids' and my wife's voices and I don't say much. However, I'd stay up late with her and talk for hours, about nothing.

Another aunt likes to drink and gamble. I'd take her to a bad casino in Summerlin, give her $100, and sit with her at a $.25 roulette table as she drank White Russians. She'd get drunk and start flirting with any guy who had the misfortune of rolling up with quarters to our table. She once took a guy's cowboy hat off, placed it over his crotch, and screamed, "The cowboy's a goner!" I don't even know what that means. Several times I wanted to shoot myself in the face. But my roulette-playing, White Russian–drinking aunt was showering my mom every morning, and I loved her for it.

My mom's best friend, Karsen, was a raging alcoholic. She was also addicted to painkillers—three years after my mom passed she was one of the 40,000 people who die from opioids each year. I'd bring her Johnnie Walker Blue Label Scotch (she usually drank Red), and we'd make Hot Pockets and wash them down with Scotch, almost every night. Karsen just wanted someone to drink with after my mom was asleep. Take your mom to the movies, go out for lunch, and take walks together. She has a tough road ahead of her being the primary caregiver for your dad.

Learning: Boundaries. Your dad's remaining days on this planet are important, and so are yours. You need to have your own life. When my mother was ill, I left every Thursday and went to NYC or Miami to keep friendships and work somewhat alive. Your accomplishments indicate your parents were able to create a positive environment to raise you in. Key to this is economic security, which at your age you need professional momentum to establish. I'd speculate your dad would appreciate you adapting your life, but not transforming it or putting your career on hold. You will likely have kids of your own, and your parents' grandkids will also need a mom who can provide for them, and feels relevant professionally. Only you can decide what this balance is.

People often outlive their prognosis. My mom was given three months but lived seven. Unfortunately, one Sunday I flew back, and she had passed 30 minutes earlier. I wish I'd been there, but would not change the approach. Had I not had some semblance of a life, I would have been less pleasant to be around (and I'm not that pleasant to begin with). It would have brought down the vibe substantially. On one of those weekends away I met someone who, two years later, I had a son with, and then another. Had I not attended to my own life, needs, and happiness, my mom likely wouldn't have grandkids.

She'd be pleased to know I have a son who looks like her, and whose middle name is Sylvia.

Learning: Shared media. My mom and I both love TV, and we watched a shit-ton together. It was awesome. *Frasier, Jeopardy!, Everybody Loves Raymond, Friends.* What's the media your dad enjoys? If it's books, read to him; music, listen together. Watch his favorite movies.

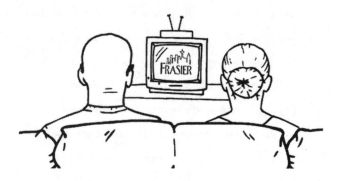

Learning: Relive his life. Looking at pictures and asking my mom to share stories from her childhood and adulthood was rewarding for us and gave her a chance to live her life again. Facilitate this as much as possible.

Learning: Nothing unsaid. Impossible to say "I love you," or how much you admire your father, too much. Impossible. I used to sit next to my mom on the couch, hold her hand, and weep and tell her how sad I was she was sick.

Learning: People will surprise and disappoint you. My mom had several close friends who never visited or even called much. It was as if they were worried they might catch her cancer. I don't think these were bad people— they just dealt with it differently. Conversely, her last boss, a successful guy 20 years younger than her, with his own family, would get on a plane every four weeks, come sit by my mom's side (where she would vomit into a plastic container every 15 minutes), and would talk to her for an hour before heading back to the airport. His name is Bob Perkowitz and he's not just successful, but kind.

Learning: It's the illness speaking. My mom was remarkably good-spirited through the process. However, it's not uncommon for people to be unreasonable, even mean, toward the end. It's the illness speaking. To the extent you can, ignore it.

What I Know

As the father of two, I can somewhat relate to your dad. I think about the end a lot so I can make better choices today. At the end, I believe parents want two things:

1. To know their family loves them immensely.

2. To recognize that their love and parenting gave their children the skills and confidence to add value and live rewarding lives.

Your message and LinkedIn profile confirm your father has achieved both these things. It must be a huge source of comfort for him to have such an impressive daughter.

Warm regards,

Scott

Love a Kid Who Isn't Your Own

FIFTY PERCENT of marriages end in divorce. Where I grew up, California, it's 60 percent. I was surrounded by stepmothers and stepfathers when I was growing up. The mother of my best friend, Adam, after her divorce, lived with a handsome, quiet law student named Paul, who mostly only spoke when it was time for me to leave. He was one of the first men I remember thinking was cool. He had awesome sunglasses and drove the coolest cars of the eighties, nineties, and aughts as his career progressed—a Datsun 260Z, a Porsche 911, and a Ferrari (I don't remember the model). He was a steady, present male role model for Adam and his sister, who, like me, only saw their biological father every other weekend.

A friend in Florida, Jimmy, is a stepdad who traded in a life as a pilot carting and partying with the wealthy around the Caribbean for a just-add-water family: wife and two school-age daughters. He boasts of his successful effort to bond with the oldest daughter by getting her into the *Wicked Tuna* series and speaks of the girls as if they're his own . . . and they are.

After my mom and dad split, I got my very own stepmom, Linda ("#3"). Dad's been married four times—my mom (#2) referred to Linda as "that bitch," as there was some overlap between #2 and #3 (see above: seventies California). I don't think my mom and Linda were ever in the same room at the same time, ever.

My mom also refused to be in the same room with my dad until my business school graduation twenty years after their divorce. The narrative was set up for me to dislike, even hate, my stepmom, Linda. One problem, though: Linda is a good person who was wonderful to me. In her twenties, Linda had been told she couldn't have children, so when a well-mannered eight-year-old boy, missing his two front teeth, showed up wearing cords and an Ocean Pacific shirt, she was in love.

Linda was the first person to spoil me. She would bake for me, a foreign concept in my house, as my mom worked and was British (not one with the kitchen). Linda would bake these amazing buckeye cookies, peanut butter paste enveloped in dark chocolate. When schedules would keep me from Linda and my dad for a month, Linda would bake buckeyes, wrap them individually in foil, and mail them to me.

One Friday she announced she was taking me to Toys"R"Us, where I could buy anything I wanted. Strolling through the aisles, she tracked my gaze and noticed me eyeing the remote control planes. She stopped me and asked which one I wanted. I was too embarrassed to say, as spending money was a crime in my household, and the planes were $30. No matter. If I wanted a model P-51 plane, she'd buy it for me—and then my father and I ventured to a parking lot and spent several hours not getting it off the ground.

Soon after, she found out that her doctors had been wrong. She was expecting. When I went to the hospital to see my half sister, Linda gave me a gift—pajamas with a picture of a basset hound with lettering underneath that read "I'm special." A dump truck on her bladder, about to push my sister through her birth canal, and Linda had found the time to get me pajamas to ensure I knew she still loved me. Some people are . . . just born wonderful.

Most mammals will give their lives defending their off-spring. What makes us human is not just opposable thumbs, but also our ability to cooperate. Cooperation draws on things that are uniquely human, like speech, culture, and long child-hoods. One of the most noble forms of cooperation that advances the species is caring for those who aren't biologically yours. I don't enjoy my kids a lot of the time, and I don't enjoy others' offspring most of the time. It's a miracle people agree to love kids who don't smell, look, or feel like them. Death, disease, and divorce leave a lot of kids in single-parent house-holds, where the odds are markedly worse for them.

The fastest blue-line path to a better world isn't economic growth or a better fucking phone, but more of us becoming irrationally passionate about the well-being of a child who isn't our own. The Pauls, Jimmys, and Lindas—being there, baking, watching bad TV, buying planes that won't fly—make us more human. My mom is gone, but this Thanksgiving my family will host Linda—my not-so-evil stepmom.

Appreciate How Fortunate You Are

I'VE BEEN thinking about AIDS a lot lately. I hope we never see an epidemic this devastating again. One million people died from AIDS-related causes in 2017, and 36 million have succumbed to the disease since the beginning of the epidemic. In sum, the HIV virus has killed the equivalent of the population of Canada.

Just as we've outsourced war to young people who feel indebted to our country—unlike an increasingly large cohort who believe the country owes them—we outsourced and compartmentalized much of the suffering and the fight against AIDS. It was a "gay disease," and we thought of a group who were victims as irresponsible instead. I believe our initial response to the crisis, as a nation, will go down as a stain on the American story.

In 1985, I remember sitting in the dining room of my fraternity and reading an *L.A. Times* article about scientists making progress toward an HIV vaccine. That meant this abstract thing called AIDS, that none of us had any contact with, was over. Only it wasn't, and all of us would know several people who'd contract HIV and ultimately die from an AIDS-related illness.

It was the perfect virus: it spread through sexual contact. Something all of us eighteen-year-old males were always thinking about and plotting. We were, theoretically, the agents and warriors for the virus. We took cold comfort believing AIDS was a disease only gay men got. And none of us knew anybody who was gay.

But we did. A bunch of us were gay. Only most, if not all, of the heterosexuals in our circle had no idea. Anybody you liked who seemed "normal" couldn't be gay, as that was a strange perversion. Definitely not anybody we knew. You couldn't be openly gay at UCLA in the eighties. It didn't matter how brave or comfortable with yourself you were. Being gay was unnatural. We were young men and women at UCLA, which was a postcard for natural and wholesome, and there was no tolerance for fucking with the postcard.

Yet this was slowly becoming the era when being gay was

tolerated. Not accepted, but tolerated. Several friends let it be known, post-graduation, that they were gay. AIDS haunted all of them, always around, waiting, striking. AIDS haunted everyone, as years earlier the blood supply had been tainted, and there was evidence this wasn't just a "gay disease." Approximately half of the nation's fifteen thousand hemophiliacs were infected. Straight people could also contract HIV. Unprotected sex meant several days of anxiety leading to 100 percent certainty you had the virus.

I've been introduced to Daniel Kahneman's notion of fast and slow thinking. Our fast, shorthand thinking offers utility but a lack of nuance. Slow thinking is where we grow and learn; it informs the fast . . . I think. College was for fast thinking. Homosexuals were "fags," and "gay" was a slur to describe something weak and unnatural. The decade after college was for slow thinking, as we discovered people we loved were gay. They had similar hopes and problems as us, only they were stalked by a plague, and their friends were dying.

After I sold my first e-commerce firm, Aardvark, my then wife and I moved from a two-bedroom in Potrero Hill to a five-bedroom in Noe Valley. That house is next to where Mark

Zuckerberg now lives. I hate myself for selling it, as (1) it's likely worth $10 million or more, and (2) I would register enormous joy sitting on my porch in a Fila tracksuit and yelling at Zuck, "How does it feel to be Putin's bitch?" But I digress. We would go to the Castro to shop for furniture to fill the five bedrooms and would see ghosts everywhere. Men in their thirties and forties who were painfully thin and had sores littering their bodies. Thirty-five-year-old men who looked eighty, barreling toward death. Ghosts, everywhere.

We like to think the time leading up to death is a period when you can reflect on a long life of blessings. It's a time to register the love you've invested and harvested. These young men were being taken early by a virus ravaging their bodies. Their backdrop: a society that had decided they weren't really victims. Not long before, we'd had a president, Reagan, who never uttered the word "AIDS" in his eight years in the White House.

Some of our friends from UCLA who contracted HIV:

- **Bill Aarons: A Lambda Chi.** Quiet, handsome kid who, we found out later, was a hemophiliac.

- **Ron Baham: Our UCLA fraternity brother.** A preppy black kid with a movie star voice.

- **Pat Williams: My UCLA freshman roommate from Visa-lia.** Pat grew up on a farm and came to UCLA to study theater. He was always chewing tobacco. He'd always borrow/steal my clothes, which was okay, as we both borrowed/stole from our other roommate, Gary.

- **Tom Bailey: My best friend Jim's partner.** A handsome guy from Atlanta who was a creative director at an ad agency, and with whom Jim fell very much in love.

Bill Aarons was the first to die. Bill contracted the virus from clotting factors made from donated blood—the treatment that had liberated him from the tyranny of a blood disorder.

Ron became a talent agent for CAA and rose to be director of current TV at Disney by the age of thirty. I saw Ron at a friend's wedding a decade after we'd graduated, and it was apparent his HIV had become full-blown AIDS. A few months later, Ron called several people he felt he needed to make amends with, mixed the contents of two dozen Valium capsules into a glass of vodka, and ingested the cocktail. Ron was dead at thirty-three.

Pat struggled with his sexuality and attended reeducation camps hosted by religious groups who felt homosexuality was learned and could be deprogrammed. Pat, someone we should have all continued to be good friends with, as we had been in college, just faded away. One of our group, a successful dentist, filled a cavity for Pat, who was in rough shape. Pat claimed he was suffering from a bad case of Lyme disease. Suffering, but still not trusting or wanting our friendship and love, as he'd seen the fast thinking at UCLA. I heard Pat died about a decade ago, but none of us are sure exactly when or where. I'm embarrassed and ashamed I didn't have the decency to track him down and tell him how impressive I thought he was (remarkably creative with boundless energy), and that I was thinking about him. I am so sorry, Pat.

Tom Bailey was caught by the warm grasp of the hand of science and has been on antiretroviral treatment for twenty years. In addition to a successful career in advertising, Tom opened a spin studio, where he was an instructor. He is the godfather to my oldest son. He's a lousy godparent. But he's healthy and married to my best friend. And that's enough.

Find Your Own Heaven

LAST WEEK, my seven-year-old son asked, "What is heaven?" I wasn't ready to give a seven-year-old my map to atheism, so I asked him what he thought heaven was. He answered, "Where you go after you die to be with your family." I'm 100 percent certain there is no God and believe that the notion of a super-being is irrational. As I've matured, I also recognize that my explanation of the universe—there was nothing, and then it exploded—is no less irrational.

As a younger man, I was always grabbing, searching. More money, more praise, more relevance, bigger, cooler experiences. But similar to the vampires in an Anne Rice novel who can have sex but never climax, there was just never enough. Until I had kids, my life was "More . . . I want fucking more." The only time I've ever felt sated, ever, is with my family.

My youngest has had trouble sleeping lately, so I meditate

with him and go through a series of stretches and exercises to clear our minds. Sensing a strategy for delaying the hour-long process of going to sleep, he asks me, any night I'm home, to "clear his mind." We go through the steps, and I finish by running my forefinger down his forehead, over his nose and lips, past his chin, and finishing on his Adam's apple. He drifts into sleep, wakes up, discovers me next to him, rolls over, flopping his outer leg and arm on me, and returns to his slumber. In that moment, "this" all makes sense: I'm with my family, watching over them, strong, timeless, immortal. My child, assessing my worth on things that have nothing to do with our modern, material world, chooses me. I'm with family, loved, and at peace. I'm in heaven.

I don't think we go to an afterworld, but I do believe we can get to heaven while still here on Earth. When I'm near the end, I want my boys and wife to lie next to me, clear my mind, run their forefingers across my forehead, and strap their arms and legs on me. This is it for me . . . I don't need anything else. I will make it to heaven, just a bit early.

Love the One(s) You're with

I WENT to my first homecoming in twenty years just recently. Berkeley, where I received my MBA, is a spectacular campus that will graduate more kids from low-income households this year than the entire Ivy League combined. They invited me to speak and offered to take me and my sons down on the field before kickoff against the University of Arizona Wildcats.

Homecoming traces its roots back to the University of Missouri, whose administrators felt it would be a good idea to host alumni back on campus. A homecoming game is usually played after the football team returns from its longest road trip and is purposefully matched against a lesser competitor so alums can feel pride in their alma mater via the most American of activities . . . crushing the competition.

I have mixed emotions visiting San Francisco and Berkeley. I had not only a different life, but a different wife . . . and feel bittersweet, including some guilt, about that time in my life. In addition, the severely mentally ill homeless dotting the sidewalks in front of buildings where twenty- and thirtysomethings aspire to aggregate the shareholder value of a small European nation as they "make the world a better place" with SaaS software and driverless cars is just fucking dystopian, in my view. I have no moral clarity here, since I was, and still am, one of them. #hypocrite

My good friend George encouraged me to go. He pointed out the importance of "taking the time to remember and visit the people and places along the way," which I thought was poetic. This emotion temporarily overrode my cynical view, developed in high school, that people who attend homecoming have already peaked, and haven't done much since.

Coming Home

What has gained more and more momentum in my life, however, is coming home. Like an Imperial TIE Fighter shooting from the bowels of the Death Star, with the tractor beam paused, I leave on business trips with a sense of determination and confidence. I am . . . On. A. Mission.

The past seven days have been a book tour with stops in Boston, Seattle, San Francisco, Los Angeles, Bentonville, and Dallas. But on the back half of every business trip, the tractor beam turns on. I can be in a galaxy far, far away, with so much still to do that I barely register it. But as I get closer, the beam's pull gets stronger and stronger, and it's as if I am falling home.

I don't think this pull will ever be greater than it is now. Having kids who are young enough to seem perfect but not old enough to recognize your imperfections creates an innocence and joy that I don't believe I'll register again until I have grand-kids. Being blessed with a great partner who also shares in this joy is the premier achievement. My students spend so much time thinking about picking the right career. However, it's a distant second relative to the mother of all important deci-sions, which will set the tone for the rest of your life (to-gether)—picking the right mate.

I didn't feel this way until I had kids. When our first son was born, I was working around the clock at L2, and used to make the three-block trek home to bathe him before going back to work.

My pace would noticeably escalate as I turned onto our block. The dopamine release you get right before seeing someone you are excited to see is one of those emotions that keeps you young. It focuses you on your better self, the self who cares about others and can't wait to be in the presence of another soul, as together, you are each a better version of yourself, a whole greater than the sum of its parts. Your family, friends, mates, and colleagues—our species thrives because of cooperation and caregiving, so our midbrain has blessed us with the steady march of happiness that washes over you when you're about to be with people you love.

I'm in the middle seat of the twenty-third row, typing with one hand, as the guy next to me is wider than his seat (normal size). Eating bad pretzels, and I am joyous. I'm in the tractor beam . . . I'm coming home.

Kids: It's All About Them

A POPULAR subject in business school is market segmentation—the process of dividing a large homogeneous market into cohorts with similar needs or wants. You then design products, pricing, and perception that match the preferences of that segment.

As marketing has evolved, managers had to figure out how to carve up the pig and sell different parts to different people,

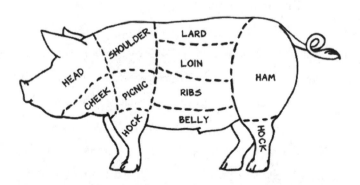

for various reasons and at varying prices, to capture surplus value. Differentiation of a product or service, real or perceived, is a form of price discrimination that helps maximize revenue while offering some consumers (twenty-one-day advance purchase and no cancellation) the chance to buy things for below cost.

Segmentation has become increasingly deft (and daft). That's not an exit row seat, but "Economy Plus," worth an incremental $29. A coach seat closer to the front will set you back $40 and includes "up to" four inches of additional pitch. You can splurge and upgrade your hotel room from a "King" to a "Superior King," which, for another $79, includes a loveseat and table.

We segment our kids into favorites. I know how awful that sounds. We naturally begin to sort, as it helps any sentient entity, or manager, achieve success—allocate resources or capital to achieve greater return than their competitors. Note: The previous sentence was a bullshit/pedantic way of saying "prioritize." I have a favorite child, always have. I think most parents do. That's the bad news. The good news is, which child that is changes back and forth. We guard the secret of who our current favorite is as if it were a nuclear launch code. Recognition that you have a favorite outs you as a terrible parent, like Steve Jobs.

I took my oldest to the World Cup, so the youngest knew he was owed, big-time. It's impressive that kids who can't put on their own pajamas understand the currency of intangibles and can communicate, super clearly, that you owe them something special. So my response to the trial attorney with his pajama top on backward: "We can do anything you want."

And then, he calls my bluff: "I want to go to Universal's Islands of Adventure *and* Volcano Bay." No. Please no. It's as if we hired a consultant to coach him on how to extract something his dad would never consider, ever, for anybody.

Orlando or Bust

We stop to get gas, and it's clear big oil has figured out segmentation. Shell gas stations segment the fuel—regular, unleaded, and supreme. I go for the supreme, as they've figured out that guys like me will pay another 27 cents per gallon because it might—who knows—be better. The two-day two-park tickets have been purchased. However, the strategy group at Comcast has found a way to extract additional 100-percent-gross-margin revenue by offering me an Express pass—cut the line for an additional $85 per ticket. Yes, I should do this. Then for another $10 ($95 total), I can purchase the "unlimited" Express pass, meaning I can cut the line on the same ride numerous times, versus just once. Who even thought of that?

They've done the testing, and anybody willing to pay $85 to cut the line is also willing to pay $95 for the same thing, but maybe a little better. In recognition of the 1 percent who have just killed it, there are now VIP private tours of theme parks with a guide who merchandises your day and escorts you through employee-only trap doors to look behind the scenes ("This is where we find phones that fall out from people on the ride above"). The cost is around $3,000 for a party of one to five people but doesn't include admission to the park. Recreation is serious business.

If this feels like a nationwide strategy to serve the cohort that has captured 85 percent of post-recession income growth

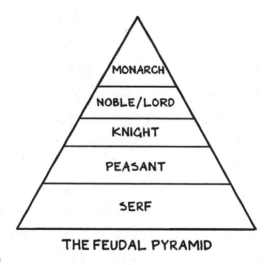

THE FEUDAL PYRAMID

SOURCE: STUDY.COM

(the top 1 percent), trust your instincts. Our economy, and its pricing, is barreling toward a society of 350 million serfs serving 3 million lords.

Potter

The Wizarding World of Harry Potter is the best product on the market, full stop. Creative attractions, great personnel, visually stunning, inspiring. The crush of humanity waiting to ride on a bookcase through Hogwarts is easy to be cynical about when you're a glass-half-empty type of guy like I am. The first day was fine. The Wizarding World was wonderful: Butterbeer and rides that are both well done and like a blast of chemo—sure to make you nauseous.

The Wizarding World has also mastered segmentation and offers Harry Potter's wand—eleven inches long, made of holly with a phoenix feather core—for $49. But wait, there's more. The wand can make crazy-cool shit happen, as wands are supposed to, when you wave one at a window in Diagon Alley. A book page turns on its own (I know, *amazing*, a page that turns on its own). However, if you want the page-turning wand, you need to purchase the stick with "interactive powers" for $59. We capped the day at the Toothsome Chocolate Emporium & Savory Feast Kitchen, which is a parent's way of saying, "I love you so much, I'll let you eat chocolate and marshmallows for dinner."

The second day was a real test: Volcano Bay. A water park designed by Neil Armstrong and Jason from *Friday the 13th*. Your TapuTapu wearable can be preloaded with your caste status. Or maybe not—we have to go to the park concierge to get another wearable in case we want to cut the line. My son and his best friend, Charlie, a wonderful boy who is happy, polite, and fearless, are leading the pack, demanding we go on everything. Charlie gives my son the confidence to go on rides he wouldn't normally, as my son would register the look of dread/terror on his dad's face and pass. But not Charlie—he's eight years old, 4 foot 2, 52 pounds, and not afraid of *anything*.

It's the end of a long day, and Dad is struggling with his inner-ear functions after the Honu ika Moana ride. It's 95 degrees of humid heat. I'm sunburned, full of Butterbeer, nauseous, and there's a decent chance I could have a stroke or start crying. It's time to go, thank Jesus. My youngest, who, again, can't put on his own pajamas, sees his opening to negotiate. "Can we go on just one more ride?"

"Sure," says Dad.

My youngest pulls out the big gun: "I want to go on the Ko'okiri Body Plunge." The plunge is a straw running down the center of an eight-story Polynesian volcano built by Polish work crews. Entrance into the straw involves climbing into a pneumatic transport tube designed for humans who decided they needed to travel down a volcano at 85 miles per hour in a dark, hermetically sealed cylinder. This is a bridge too far for me. So, after validating that they are tall enough, Dad sends them up the 476 steps and agrees to meet them at the pool that Ko'okiri expectorates them into. In essence, I leave all parenting decisions to a painted sign that, because my son is tall enough, assures me I no longer need to be his guardian. Good stuff.

I walk to the volcano's urinal, the exit pool, but too much time goes by. Where's my boy? Is he in the capsule, stuck and screaming? Would he not get in the capsule, and is hovering around the top of the straw wondering where his dad is? Finally, his friend explodes into the pool and seems only mildly scarred by the experience. So, I think, my boy must be plunging through the volcano, at 1/10th the speed of sound. I try to remain calm but am worried sick. I mean, sick.

Standing at the edge of the pool, I wait for my son. And then my eight-year-old, who survived the plunge and is my favorite again, comes barreling into the water. His dad, in a bathing suit, Havaianas flip-flops, and dress socks (forgot athletic socks and was worried my feet were getting sunburned), is there armed with reassurance ("That was amazing, so proud of you!") and a protein bar ("Are you hungry?").

He is rattled by the violent drop of the Ko'okiri, but his gaze immediately finds his dad, and he looks relieved, even gratified. He has dropped eight stories, feels a sense of accomplishment, and asks to go again. He knows he can do it, and that a man in shorts and dress socks will be at the bottom waiting for him. Someone who loves him, completely.

Love Unconditionally

There are so few absolutes. The theory of competitive advantage, diversification, karma, the wisdom of crowds are all things I thought were absolutes but that have been disproven. Is there any one truism I would feel (almost) 100 percent confident that you will find not just return but reward from your investment?

Spoiler alert: It's love. However, there is nuance. Getting to a place, economically, emotionally, and spiritually, where you can love someone completely, without expecting anything in return, is the absolute.

The universe chooses prosperity and progress. When a universe loses its source of all life, the sun, it also triggers a cosmic process to birth a new, better sun. As the universe chooses progress, it creates incentives that result in a natural progression upward. Over the long term, markets go up, and each generation gets taller.

The incentive is that the actions to foment progress are rewarding, so as to keep us eating, having sex, and loving. The most important act of progress for our species, planet, and universe is unconditional love. The cosmos recognizes this and rewards this behavior with the deepest meaning and well-being that any of us can register.

As an atheist, I believe this is it. That when I'm near the end, I'll look into my kids' eyes and know our relationship is almost over. And that's okay, as it motivates me. A recognition of the finite nature of life is a blessing, as it focuses you on loving, forgiving, and pursuing.

Health

Be Strong

As Dr. Henry S. Lodge says, we are hunter-gatherers and are happiest when in motion and surrounded by others. As referenced earlier, a decent proxy for your success will be your ratio of sweating to watching others sweat (watching sports on TV). It's not about being ripped, but committing to being strong physically and mentally. The trait most common among CEOs is that they exercise regularly. Walking into any conference room and believing that, if shit got real, you could kill and eat the others gives you an edge and confidence. (Note: Don't do this.)

On a regular basis, at work, demonstrate both your physical and mental strength—your grit. Work an eighty-hour week, be the calm one in the face of stress, attack a big problem with sheer brute force and energy. People will notice. At Morgan Stanley, the analysts pulled all-nighters weekly, and it didn't kill us, but made us stronger. As you get older, however, this approach to work can in fact kill you. So do it now.

6 Foot 2, 187 Pounds: My Height, Weight

My height and weight and general strength are a big source of focus for me, as I was painfully skinny growing up. When I arrived at UCLA, I was 6 foot 3, 138 pounds. Joining the crew team and having access to three meals a day (via Jeanne, the cook at ZBT fraternity) resulted in thirty new pounds of muscle. Soon after the weight gain, women started noticing me—which was awesome. Since then, I've associated strength and muscle with worth as a mate. I'm losing muscle strength and haven't found other sources of security and worth. I'm struggling with this whole aging thing.

Don't Sweat the Small Stuff. Or the Big Stuff.

I'm increasingly aware of my mood, heartbeat, and blood pressure as I get older. Recently I was at the Founders Forum (a conference for entrepreneurs and founders) in London. When I arrived, I discovered I wasn't speaking at a plenary session, but at one of two concurrent sessions. My competition was

Jean Liu, the president of DiDi, the Chinese ride-hailing firm. It gets worse. Liu was scheduled in "Amber," a room bigger than "Cedar," where I was speaking. My inner jackal voice immediately registered this as a grave injustice.

It's the most impressive gathering of this type I've been to in a while. I arrived at 2 p.m., having eaten nothing. I'd been stressed lately, and when I get stressed, I forget to eat. I was starting to feel faint, so I wolfed down two lattes and an apple seven minutes before going onstage, where I proceeded to yell at the audience and didn't stop yelling for thirty minutes and 143 slides. About twenty minutes in, there was feedback on the sound system, and I began to have PVCs (premature ventricular contractions—irregular heartbeats). The bad thing about my irregular beats isn't just that they are irregular, but that I can feel them, which freaks me out.

The feedback, burst of PVCs, and two hundred people staring up at me took my heart rate way up. I tried to calm myself by looking at the bright side: if I collapsed and died onstage, I'd get a shit-ton of views on YouTube.

As I've gotten older, I'm able to separate the small things from the big things and not sweat the little stuff. The previous sentence is a lie. Similar to jet lag and hangovers, the impact of stress on me has worsened with age. I'd describe myself as a dope sleepwalking through the first forty years of my life. It had its upsides. The problem with being more thoughtful as you get older is that you actually think about shit. My life is easy compared to the billions of people who have trouble putting food on the table or who struggle with illness, but stress gets to me nonetheless.

Off the Rails

Over the last five years, I've given about four hundred talks, and around 1 percent of the time, it all comes off the rails. I become anxious, start sweating, and my voice starts to shake. I begin gulping for oxygen and feel as if I am going to throw up and pass out. My talk "The Four Horsemen" at the DLD (Digital-Life-Design) conference in Munich went viral (for an academic, anyway). That set in motion a bunch of great things for L2: a book deal, inbound inquiries, increased awareness of the firm. I now give the opening address each year at DLD. But at DLD15, out of nowhere . . . an attack. I came close to passing out onstage and had to lean over with my hands on my knees for thirty seconds. The nice folks at DLD wanted to take me to the hospital, as they were convinced I was having a cardiac event. Good stuff. By the way, the talk received 1.1 million views on YouTube. Apparently my near stroke was less obvious to viewers—few mentions in the comments. Another example of nothing ever being as good, or bad, as it seems at the time.

Another time, I was set to appear on Fox to discuss Trump's attacks on Amazon when I received an email that the president's recently appointed chief economic adviser, Larry Kudlow, would also be appearing in the segment. I started to get anxious. I then noticed my outfit. For some reason I had put everything in my closet on my person, including a hoodie, and was wearing about eleven layers.

Fight-or-flight set in, and I began strategizing on how to head this feeling off at the pass. "I know, I'll have a drink . . . it will calm my nerves." I'm pretty sure this is what most clinicians call alcoholism. It wasn't my fear of descending into full-blown substance abuse that stopped me from shotgunning one or two Lagunitas IPAs at the nearest deli, but the prospect of somebody seeing me downing beers at 9:45 in the morning in Midtown. In short, I didn't, and I was okay. I took beta-blockers for a while, which appeared to cure it. However, I don't want to become reliant on any substance to perform. Unless, of course, it's Lunesta, caffeine, Cialis, Chipotle, or cannabis. Or as I refer to them, the five food groups. If I weren't an atheist, it would be reasonable to think it's God reminding me I'm just not that cool. However, as an atheist, I'm pretty sure these are panic attacks, the source of which I'll figure out . . . never.

Cry—It's Good for You

CRYING MAY have an evolutionary purpose, as it signals surrender ("please stop what you are doing to me"), elicits empathy from those around you, and can help parents locate their offspring. For babies, active crying may be a way of restoring equilibrium after overstimulation. One way to solve this is to mimic the womb with the 5 S's—swaddle, side-stomach position, shush, swing, suck—a method developed by Dr. Harvey Karp. (That. Shit. Is. Genius. I'd seriously consider having a third kid, if babies weren't so awful, just for the chance to impress childless friends with the 5 S's.) Crying can also relieve the stress brought on by an onslaught of emotions that are difficult to process. Men aren't supposed to cry, which likely is a function of the whole "indicates surrender" thing.

The Partridge Family

The first time I remember crying, I mean really crying, was at age nine. My mom had left my dad and me (she came back two weeks later to get me). I was watching *The Partridge Family* with my dad, on a Friday night at 8:30, pre-DVR. We were sitting on the couch in matching orange terrycloth robes, the height of opulence in 1970s middle-class America. My dad had received these luxury items as swag for playing in a golf tournament hosted by his firm, ITT. He snagged a size small for me, which was still eight sizes too big for a nine-year-old. Embroidered on the chest of our Tang-colored slouchwear was a red flagstick above green cursive that read "Pebble Beach." I didn't know where Pebble Beach was, but I knew important people played golf there, which meant my dad was important.

I hadn't registered the shit that had gone down two weeks previous, but it suddenly crept up on me and, draped in my Turkish cotton tent, I began to sob uncontrollably. I cried for a good thirty minutes. My dad seemed panicked and kept saying, "I'm so sorry, is there anything I can do?" I would respond, "No, I'm just sad." That was our first real conversation.

I lost the capacity to cry for about ten years between ages thirty-four and forty-four. Didn't cry when I got divorced or when my mom died. Just forgot how, I think. I'm obsessed with business, am hugely stressed over it, and wrap way too much of my identity and self-worth around professional success. But I've never cried because of business. And trust me, there has been good reason several (hundred) times. However, since my mid-forties, something strange:

I cry all the time.

Pretty sure it's a good thing. Sorrowful crying is looking to the past with sadness or to the future with dread. Crying as a result of happiness is a response to a moment as if it's eternal; the person is frozen in a blissful, immortalized present. My tears lately (thankfully) have been the latter, as I slow down and pursue moments. Moments with friends, moments trying to freeze time with my kids, and (mostly) feeling very in the moment watching movies and TV. At least a third of the episodes of *Modern Family* get me weepy, and something about being on a plane turns me into a mess. (Do not watch the movie *Gleason* on a plane.)

I also choke up in class more often, in front of 170 kids in their late twenties. I used to feel embarrassed and tell myself I needed to keep it together. But as we get older we become more like ourselves, and I'm getting more comfortable with raw emotions and the potential collateral damage. I've earned it. As you get older and begin to register the finite time you have, you want to freeze time and have moments when you feel something.

Most depression isn't feeling sad, but feeling nothing. Crying, especially in the company of, or while thinking about, loved ones, feels healthy and joyous. I well up just thinking about it.

Trade Closeness for Harmony

MY FAMILY—my dad, sister, and I—are not close by American standards. No BBQs, daily calls, or watching sports together. However, I'll trade closeness for harmony . . . and we have a lot of that. My friends who have uber-close but dysfunctional relationships with their families are often exhausted for the wrong reasons. The three of us are low maintenance, no-drama, and additive to each other's lives. An unexpected bonus is, in addition to loving each other, we like each other—we get along well.

Every few years for the last two decades, we've gone to Cabo, which my dad loves. This time, however, was harder. My dad is eighty-eight and has lost a lot of weight recently. His leg muscles have atrophied, as they do, and he is having trouble walking. Our dad had been "that guy" who never seemed to age, so him requiring assistance to get around is rattling. Some of his most treasured items are medals for placing first in his age group (fifties) in several 10K races. He's especially fond of one photo showing him on the medals podium celebrating his victory with a cigarette.

Both my sister and I have worked out three-plus times a week since we were eighteen. Our chain-smoking, 10K-medalist father got us exercising in our teens, and it stuck. We will all need help walking at some point, but that day will likely come years later for my sister and me than for most people, thanks to him.

The highlight of each trip is the three of us beachside drinking our dinner. The conversation inevitably turns to my dad's ex-wives (three of them), my sister's ex-boyfriends (guys who all lit up a room by leaving it), and my neuroses (numerous). None of these on their own are that interesting, but with several margaritas they. Are. All. Fucking. Hilarious. As cell death occurs, and it does for 100 percent of us, either cognitive or physical impairment sets in. We spend most of our time stationary, so having our dad ageless at eighty-eight (alert, funny) while seated makes it obvious you want your legs to go before your memory.

Be a Caregiver

Caregivers live longer than any cohort, and the number of people you love and care for is the strongest signal about how long you'll live. Like many men, I haven't really provided much care for many people. I spend a lot of time with my kids, but their mom is their primary caregiver. My caregiving is watching Premier League highlights, taking them to hibachi, and asking Alexa questions about *Star Wars* (never gets old). Getting my dad to and from Cabo and around a hotel—a stark reminder of how awesome government regulation is (Americans with Disabilities Act)—is the most real caregiving I've done since my mom was sick. You can feel the benefits. It's taxing, but rewarding. You have to be engaged and organized (key to brain health), and you feel you have purpose—in this case, making sure my dad didn't fall.

I told my dad it was time to start getting wheelchair service at airports, and he was cool, even Zen, about it. Being wheeled through security, he seemed relieved not to have to think about all the bullshit we endure on the other side of the metal detector—*Which bag is mine? Where are my shoes? Fuck . . . do I have a vape pen in my carry-on?* In front of us was someone else in a wheeled vehicle, a two-year-old girl. She wasn't nearly as Zen as my dad with the whole being pushed around thing— she was screaming.

All of us share strollers and wheelchairs in our past/future. We put people on wheels so they can be with us when we venture from home, and mobility is something so wonderful we pull it forward and extend it. The little girl was upset, as little kids get, and was clearly not convinced the wheels were a function of people caring about her. My dad, however, knows this is true.

Get Lost in the Moment

THE FASTEST-GROWING demographic is centenarians. How can you live to be one hundred? Easy. Have good genetics, live a healthy lifestyle, and love others. Loving is the bomb when it comes to living. We like to think genetics are number one, so we can abdicate responsibility for abusing our bodies, since "the die has been cast." No, it hasn't.

There's an x factor, things outside our control that can deliver tragedy for no reason. My first summer share in the Hamptons was with two women—one a mother to infant twins—who died in their early forties from cancer within a year of each other. As we get older, we encounter more x factor, like people dying when they shouldn't. As a result, we begin adjusting other algorithms.

Tomorrow vs. Today

Stanford professor Walter Mischel studied delayed gratification, offering children a small reward: one marshmallow—or two marshmallows, if they didn't eat the first one after being left alone with it. The study tracked the kids, and those with the discipline to leave the first marshmallow alone were more successful later in life. Our education system and culture focus on getting kids to be little gratification delayers. Few parents scream at their kids, "I need you to be more in the moment!" But as we get older, and encounter more x factor, we start wondering, "Why am I so fucking stressed today, trying to build a better tomorrow, when I'm equally stressed the next day? When does tomorrow, the reward, become today?"

I'm (desperately) trying to be more in the moment and have found that it's a real effort. Unless I'm with my kids, who demand that it be all about today . . . and that's usually whatever they need or want at that moment. A good thing. Recently a flight I was waiting for to London was delayed, so I started making calls, reading email, doing work. And then I thought . . . *fuck it*. I went to duty free and bought a bunch of cured ham (when in Rome). Went to a bar, ordered a pilsner, put on my noise-canceling headphones, and blared Calvin Harris as I ate pork. I. Love. Pork. I could shower in the other white meat.

Super "in the moment," I headed to the gate, walked through some imposing glass doors, but no gates on the other side, just a baggage carousel. WTF. I had just—somehow—left the terminal and the secure area. There's a reason you feel recalcitrant walking past the point-of-no-return TSA guy, as—and I can attest to this—they will not let you back in. In an instant, I had missed my plane. Which put me. In. The. Moment.

We're all seeking that balance . . . that sweet spot. Delaying gratification, so we can build a better tomorrow for us, our family, and others. You can't miss too many planes, as people on the other end are counting on you. But there is value to waving your middle finger at the x factor, getting lost in pork, and missing a few.

Don't Be an Asshole

I'VE BEEN thinking about emotional and mental health lately. What makes kids and dogs so captivating on camera (actors feel upstaged by kids and pets) is they're 100 percent authentic.

Your kids don't worry that lying on top of you during *Outrageous Acts of Science* will be inappropriate or unwelcome. Affection from offspring is immensely rewarding, as it's raw—no objective, no expectation, no filter. Just a natural urge to feel your warmth and be closer to you—someone they love and who loves them.

My oldest reinforces this authenticity when several minutes later he declines the offer to wash the car with me. He'd rather play FIFA 18. Yesterday, our seven-year-old told us he "feels love" when he touches his wenis (his name for it, not ours) and when he sees dogs. His brother, who never agrees with him, nodded as if this were a universal truth.

School, discipline, and parenting are mostly about constructing filters so your kids stay in their swim lanes, stay out of jail, fit in, and chart a path toward a true north. Teens, around their parents, become experts at filtering everything you say and finding all the impurities in everything you do. Everything. As we spill into adulthood, we develop more filters in dating, at college, at work.

There is a freedom and cathartic release, as you get older, to tolerating cracks in the filters, making them more porous, your actions and words more genuine. My filters had little problem expanding at work and with service employees. I've been incredibly open with people who didn't perform up to my expectations, the standards for the job, or the cab fare. Direct, constructive feedback is valuable.

But my "feedback" has been the (non)gift that keeps on giving. Always quick to remind the guy—who's probably supporting three kids on $40,000 a year—that it took forty minutes to get my room service. Or expecting that if I'm working at midnight, the twenty-four-year-old who works for me should be as well. I try to compensate for the former by tipping generously, but that's paying it backward—I worked my way through high school and college (as a waiter, valet, and busboy) and see my-self in every service worker. But 25 percent is no excuse for being a jerk. Trying to fix this.

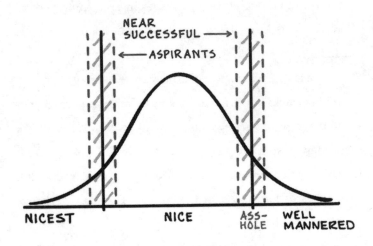

I've been around enormously successful people since a young age, mostly through work, and I have known many on a personal level. There is an arc to being an asshole. The aspi-rants (people trying to make a living) are generally nice and not expectant. I don't know if it's the humility you develop not having reached economic security, fear of pissing off the wrong gal or guy, values, or if it's reflexive, as many spend time in the service industry. The near successful (where I've spent most of my adult life) tend to overindex on the asshole meter, as our insecurity and anger at not having made the jump to light speed can turn to expectations and actions that vainly attempt to highlight what a big fucking deal I am.

The super-successful people I know are usually nicer, more generous, and generally better mannered. The billionaire jerk portrayed in movies and on TV is mostly a cartoon—an animation of something that isn't real. I'd like to think generosity and manners are a signal and cause of success. But I believe manners are also a function of other factors: (1) Billionaires have more to lose. Being a jerk to an Uber driver when you're the CEO of Uber can and should cost you billions (and it did). And (2) you take stock of your blessings and have an easier time being less of an asshole. One of the nice things about aging is that while some filters are renewing ("Do I really need to criticize this person?"), others are coming down, making it easy and natural to compliment others.

Praise Others

I'm 100 percent certain there is no god. At least not the Morgan Freeman/Lifetime/Fox version of God. However, I do pray. Just as writing down your goals makes them more likely to come to fruition, being grateful has been proven to increase health and life expectancy. In psychology research, gratitude is consistently correlated with greater happiness. Gratitude helps people feel more positive emotions, relish life's experiences, improve their health, deal with adversity, and build strong relationships.

Writing about your aspirations and articulating all the things you're grateful for is a form of prayer. I'm more committed to prayer in the company of others—being transparent about my objectives and expressing gratitude. Or, more often, being specific about how impressive the other person is. As a younger man, I felt that complimenting other men was somehow a zero-sum game. That acknowledging their achievements and attributes took away from mine. So small.

Time with my boys and exercising have been effective antidepressants. Increasingly, I'm adding a third: prayer in the form of appreciation/admiration. It's not charity, as it makes me feel important, healthy, and confident to praise others. There's still a long way to go, as my old insecurities die hard.

We all have good intentions that don't lead to action. We have an even greater reservoir of admiration and good thoughts about others that get caught in the filters of insecurity and fear. To not let that dam burst is to cut life short and shortchange joy. There are so few absolutes. One of them: Nobody ever says at a funeral, "He was too generous, too kind, and much too loving."

Nobody. Ever.

Sustenance > Addictive Substances

WHEN A rat presses a lever and gets a treat, predictably, every time, the rat will return to the lever when it's hungry. But if you start varying the reward—no sugary snack for several tries, and then maybe three fall after the lever is pushed—then the rat will remain at the lever tapping uncontrollably. Random, unpredictable rewards are the stuff of addiction.

I'm addicted to Twitter or, more likely, to the reaffirmation I get from the microblogging platform. However, there is no free lunch with addiction. The hangover for me, after wrapping the pursuit of truth (what all academics are supposed to do) in the sensationalism that sells, is that I feel empty and a bit pathetic. Why is a fifty-four-year-old professor of marketing even on Twitter?

The Arm on the Slot Machine

We unwittingly pull the arm of a slot machine every day. Our youngest, eight years old, usually stumbles into our room for the last hour of his sleep. There are few things (maybe heroin?) that can turn from so wonderful to so awful in three minutes. When he rests on me, I am whole . . . and everything makes sense. I drift back to sleep knowing I matter. Despite mattering, three minutes later my medulla oblongata wakes me, as I'm near asphyxiation. I need to get this 57-pound sack of flesh off my chest or I'll die—and he (I think/hope) would be scarred by waking up on top of his dead dad. I might sell the idea to the Hallmark Channel. But I digress.

So now he's up. His mom and dad sit in dopamine-filled anticipation as his senses light up and begin processing. Looking around, hair so disheveled it's extraordinary, the spinning wheels of perception whirring, absorbing the new world the day may bring. He's deciding if it's a good day. *Hey, there's Dad, and he loves me, and I love him so much I'll flop on him again and lie still for fifteen seconds radiating happiness.* Then he pops up and informs us he's headed downstairs to find his best friend, his brother.

Or—and this is the key to the dopamine, as there seems to be no discernible pattern—he senses there's something bad about today. In three seconds, the suspicion turns to certainty. Yes, definitely, the day ahead is a force of evil threatening all that's good in the world, and his ferociously bad attitude is the key weapon to be deployed.

The spawn of Satan begins whining and picking fights posed as questions: "Do I have to go to soccer?" "Can I have gummy bears for breakfast?" The rest of the day turns into a hostage situation where I long for the days of Bing Crosby, when hitting your kids was not only acceptable but good parenting. And then, out of nowhere . . . the terrorist in Iron Man pajamas sits next to me and begins rubbing my head and laughing at the way it feels, and asking me questions about my mom. "Did she look like you? Did you live in a big house?"

In addition to video games, my kids are developing other dopamine loops, and it's interesting to see them unfold. Last weekend my youngest came into our bedroom and took his place between his mom and dad. I noticed him clinging to a large spherical object and assumed it was a stuffed Angry Bird. I eased the object from my son's hands and, in the dark, made out an "8" on the sphere. He had a Magic 8 Ball and was sleeping with it.

Later that morning, my Hallmark Channel son showed up and decided we should ask the most important questions of the all-knowing M8B:

- **"Will Dad ever get his hair back?"** Answer: Outlook not so good (hard to explain how hilarious my eight-year-old found this).
- **"Will Mommy buy me FIFA 18?"** Answer: Better not tell you now.

For three days my son walked around clinging to his M8B. Addicted to random rewards and feedback.

The unpredictability, immediate feedback, and variability of rewards, coupled with a genetic predisposition to fixate on your kids so the species continues, make kids an addictive substance to their parents. I spend much of the week in New York, away from them. By Thursday, I'm feeling antsy and depressed. Need my fix.

Food, sex, and kids. We're wired to be addicted to things fundamental to the survival of the species. I trust that my boys will recognize that their mom and dad did not offer the dopamine hit of an addictive substance, but instead offered sustenance. We are always here, predictable. We're a sure thing, wired to love them no matter what, and we present this love with less variance than any other relationship. Will my sons remember that we, while not perfect, were always there?

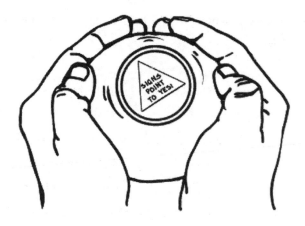

Epilogue

In the end, relationships
are all that matters.

MY MOM met her best friend, Karsen Evans, in the secretarial pool of the ITT office in Orange County. Karsen was funny and outgoing, and bore a striking resemblance to Ann-Margret. She married a successful entrepreneur, Charly, who owned a printing business. Karsen and Charly were dear friends to my mom. She stayed with them after she and my dad split.

In their company, as a nine-year-old, I registered several things for the first time:

1. Karsen was the first woman I remember thinking was really "pretty."
2. I noticed they had nicer things than we did: a big house overlooking the Valley, German cars, fur coats, and fancy guns from Italy. Karsen wore a belt with gold hoops that encased twenty-four $10 Indian Head Gold

Eagle coins. Karsen and Charly were something I had never encountered or noticed before. They were "rich."

3. They also didn't have kids, and had fun parties where groovy people got drunk. They would dance to a live band whose lead singer Charly knew personally. They were "cool."

In high school, Charly would take me to lunch at his firm, and I began to get a sense of work and what it meant to make money. I started to connect work with gold coins and groovy people who listened to live music, overlooking the San Fernando Valley.

Charly was ahead of his time. He saw disruption coming and made a bold bet on technology—computers that would replace typesetting. The technology was not practical and required him to change the entire operation of his company at huge costs. Within two years, his firm of thirty years was out of business, and Charly and Karsen were financially ruined. As in many marriages, financial strain spelled doom, and Karsen told Charly she was leaving him.

Soon after, Charly was admitted to the hospital with what was then called a nervous breakdown. The term *depression* wasn't yet part of American vocabulary. After being discharged from the hospital, Charly asked Karsen to go the grocery store, as they were out of Häagen-Dazs. Once she left, Charly went into the garage, put shells in an antique rifle, pressed the muzzle to his chest, and pulled the trigger. Four hundred people came to the funeral—he was loved. I remember the juxtaposition of more than a hundred people crying, his three grown sons (from his first marriage) sobbing uncontrollably, and Karsen, wearing thigh-high leather boots, welcoming everyone.

Soon after Charly passed, Karsen had several failed back surgeries and became addicted to opioids. She and my mom remained close. When my mom was sick, Karsen showed up unexpectedly on my mom's doorstep one day and announced she was there to take care of her best friend. She had driven from San Diego to Las Vegas. I unloaded her canary-yellow Corvette of its contents: two fake Vuitton bags, a Maltese dog, and seven one-liter bottles of Johnnie Walker Red.

When my mom became really ill, Karsen would help her with things I couldn't—showering, changing. She made Hot Pockets for us every night. She would also seduce thirtysomething maintenance workers (my mom lived on a golf course) and drank a liter of Scotch every three or four days. By this math, I figured Karsen had given my mom a month to live, as that's when Karsen would run out of Red Label.

After my mom died, Karsen asked if I would look in on her. I called once a month for about six months, and then stopped calling. I got too wrapped up in my own shit to call the woman who had showered my mom when she was dying. So selfish.

I got a call two years later that Karsen had died. Unable to get a ride to pick up her pain meds, she experienced serious withdrawal, and her heart gave out. Her estate attorney informed me

I was the sole beneficiary of her estate (using the term generously). Still, more than I deserved. Just like referred pain, this was love for my mom manifesting somewhere else.

I inherited the belt of Gold Eagles and decided to keep them in case shit got real—end-of-the-world stuff. I could hitchhike to Idaho and begin trading gold coins for guns, butter, and a few days in someone's underground bunker. You never know.

I hid the belt, which is a bad idea, as a third of the things I don't hide I lose anyway. I hadn't seen the coins in several years when my close friend Adam asked if I knew there was costume jewelry, a tacky gold belt, in a dresser I had given him. I told him it wasn't costume and that it was likely worth tens of thousands of dollars. Adam said his thirteen-year-old son had been wearing it to seventh grade every day as a necklace, because it made him look like a rapper. He gave it back to me.

Karsen and Charly Evans were the most impressive people we knew, on top of the world, and they both died alone. Karsen was an addict whose only family or friend was my mom. Charly was too sick to feel the love of his family. I've become an addict of sorts as well. Addicted to the affirmation and economic security that comes with professional success. I look at the belt and feel the need to invest in relationships in case they are all I'm left with, and to maintain the perspective that, in the end, that is all we have, and all that matters.

Acknowledgments

IT WAS rewarding to get the band back together for this book. My agent, Jim Levine, keeps me (mostly) in line and is a constant source of support and inspiration. My editor, Niki Papadopoulos, will be a veterinarian in her next life, as she is strong yet gentle. In this life, she kept me and the work on track.

My colleague Katherine Dillon is my professional rock, and Kyle Scallon spent evenings and weekends helping these concepts come to life. Maria Petrova uses her fourth-language skills to make my first and only language go down much easier.

Beata, thanks for bringing happiness and joy to our house every day. I love you.

Notes

INTRODUCTION

12. **in your fifties:** Ingraham, Christopher. "Under 50? You Still Haven't Hit Rock Bottom, Happiness-wise." *Wonkblog* (blog), *Washington Post*, August 24, 2017. https://www.washington post.com/news/wonk/wp/2017/08/24/under-50-you-still-havent-hit-rock-bottom-happiness-wise.

12. **Happiness is waiting:** Clinical depression is something I do not have the expertise to address.

15. **sweats every day:** Cohen, Jennifer. "Exercise Is One Thing Most Successful People Do Everyday." *Entrepreneur*, June 6, 2016. https://www.entrepreneur.com/article/276760.

18. **source of marital acrimony:** Rampell, Catherine. "Money Fights Predict Divorce Rates." *Economix* (blog), *New York Times*, December 7, 2009. https://economix.blogs.nytimes.com/2009/12/07/money-fights-predict-divorce-rates.

19. **We have a caste system:** Carnevale, Anthony P., Tamara Jayasundera, and Artem Gulish. *America's Divided Recovery:*

College Haves and Have-Nots. Georgetown University Center on Education and the Workforce, 2016. https://cew.georgetown.edu/cew-reports/americas-divided-recovery.

19. **handful of supercities:** Khanna, Parag. "How Much Economic Growth Comes from Our Cities?" World Economic Forum, April 13, 2016. https://www.weforum.org/agenda/2016/04/how-much-economic-growth-comes-from-our-cities.

20. **the correlation flattens:** Martin, Emmie. "Here's How Much Money You Need to Be Happy, According to a New Analysis by Wealth Experts." CNBC Make It, November 20, 2017. https://www.cnbc.com/2017/11/20/how-much-money-you-need-to-be-happy-according-to-wealth-experts.html.

21. **Being "in the zone" is happiness**: Csikszentmihalyi, Mihaly. 2004. "Flow, the Secret to Happiness." Filmed February 2004 in Monterey, CA. TED video, 18:55. https://www.ted.com/talks/mihaly_csikszentmihalyi_on_flow.

22. **money early and often:** Hafner, Peter. "The Top 3 Benefits of Investing in the Markets Early." *Active/Passive*, CNBC, September 12, 2017. https://www.cnbc.com/2017/09/12/the-top-3-benefits-of-investing-in-the-markets-early.html.

23. **The app 1 Second Everyday:** 1 Second Everyday home page, https://1se.co.

24. **more social bonds:** Schülke, Oliver, Jyotsna Bhagavatula, Linda Vigilant, and Julia Ostner. "Social Bonds Enhance

Reproductive Success in Male Macaques." *Current Biology* 20 (December 21, 2010): 2207–10. https://bit.ly/2vvjq95.

26. **Harvard Medical School Grant Study:** Mineo, Liz. "Good Genes Are Nice, but Joy Is Better." *Harvard Gazette*, April 2017. https://news.harvard.edu/gazette/story/2017/04/over-nearly-80-years-harvard-study-has-been-showing-how-to-live-a-healthy-and-happy-life.

28. **people overestimate the amount of happiness:** Norton, Amy. "People Overestimate the Happiness New Purchases Will Bring." HealthDay.com, January 25, 2013. https://consumer.healthday.com/mental-health-information-25/behavior-health-news-56/people-overestimate-the-happiness-new-purchases-will-bring-672626.html.

29. **the joy of children:** Mosher, Dave. "Holding a Baby Can Make You Feel Bodaciously High—and It's a Scientific Mystery." *Business Insider*, November 15, 2016, https://www.businessinsider.com/baby-bonding-oxytocin-opioids-euphoria-2016-10.

32. **keys to a healthy relationship:** Firestone, Lisa. "Forgiveness: The Secret to a Healthy Relationship." *Huffington Post*, October 15, 2015. https://www.huffpost.com/entry/forgiveness-the-secret-to-a-healthy-relationship_b_8282616.

SUCCESS

39. **able to provide:** Vo, Lam Thuy. "How Much Does It Cost to Raise a Child?" *Wall Street Journal*, June 22, 2016. http://blogs.wsj.com/economics/2016/06/22/how-much-does-it-cost-to-raise-a-child.

39. **kid in Manhattan:** Fishbein, Rebecca. "It Could Cost You $500K to Raise a Child in NYC." *Gothamist*, August 19, 2014. http://gothamist.com/2014/08/19/condoms_4life.php.

39. **must have Manhattan private schools:** Anderson, Jenny and Rachel Ohm. "Bracing for $40,000 at New York City Private Schools," *New York Times*, January 29, 2012, http://www.nytimes.com/2012/01/29/nyregion/scraping-the-40000-ceiling-at-new-york-city-private-schools.html.

43. **bright-light visions people describe:** Pollan, Michael. *How to Change Your Mind: What the New Science of Psychedelics Teaches Us About Consciousness, Dying, Addiction, Depression, and Transcendence*. New York: Random House, 2018.

49. **One article on the exchange:** "Get Your Sh** Together: NYU Professor's Response to Student Who Complained After He Was Dismissed from Class for Being an Hour Late Takes Web by Storm." *Daily Mail*, April 14, 2013. https://www.dailymail.co.uk/news/article-2308827/Get-sh-t-NYU-professors-response-student-complained-dismissed-class-hour-late.html.

56. **the original gangster of cable:** "#67 John Malone." *Forbes,* January 15, 2019. https://www.forbes.com/profile/john-malone/#349608415053.

57. **You're a fraud:** Richards, Carl. "Learning to Deal with the Impostor Syndrome." *Your Money* (blog), *New York Times,* October 26, 2015. https://www.nytimes.com/2015/10/26/your-money/learning-to-deal-with-the-impostor-syndrome.html.

58. **Seventy percent of Americans:** Page, Danielle. "How Impostor Syndrome Is Holding You Back at Work." *Better* (blog), NBC News, October 26, 2017. https://www.nbcnews.com/better/health/how-impostor-syndrome-holding-you-back-work-ncna814231.

58. **they get louder:** Vozza, Stephanie. "It's Not Just You: These Super Successful People Suffer from Impostor Syndrome." *Fast Company,* August 9, 2017. https://www.fastcompany.com/40447089/its-not-just-you-these-super-successful-people-suffer-from-imposter-syndrome.

66. **is being born in America:** Galloway, Scott. "Enter Uber." *Daily Insights,* Gartner L2, June 16, 2017. https://www.l2inc.com/daily-insights/no-mercy-no-malice/enter-uber.

73. **every five to seven years:** Sundby, Alex. "Bank Execs Offer Head-Scratching Answers." CBS News, January 14, 2010. http://www.cbsnews.com/news/bank-execs-offer-head-scratching-answers.

74. **An asset bubble:** Kleintop, Jeffrey. "Where's the Next Bubble?" *Market Commentary* (blog), Charles Schwab, July 10, 2017. https://www.schwab.com/resource-center/insights/content/where-s-the-next-bubble

74. **nearing a full-monty bubble:** "5 Steps of a Bubble." *Insights* (blog), Investopedia, June 2, 2010. http://www.investopedia.com/articles/stocks/10/5-steps-of-a-bubble.asp.

74. **between 1999 and 2019:** "Brad McMillan: Similarities Between 2017 and 1999," June 30, 2017, in *Your Money Briefing*. Podcast, MP3 audio, 5:55. http://www.wsj.com/podcasts/brad-mcmillan-similarities-between-2017-and-1999/0EB5C970-1D74-4D6C-A7C8-1C8D7D08EC8B.html.

76. **Kids who can code:** "25 Best Paying Cities for Software Engineers," Glassdoor. https://www.glassdoor.com/blog/25-best-paying-cities-software-engineers.

77. **They are also competing with the Four:** Galloway, Scott. *The Four.* New York: Portfolio, 2017. https://www.penguinrandomhouse.com/books/547991/the-four-by-scott-galloway.

77. **superblocks in NYC:** Gustin, Sam. "Google Buys Giant New York Building for $1.9 Billion." *Wired*, December 22, 2010, https://www.wired.com/2010/12/google-nyc.

77. **World Economic Forum's annual meeting:** "An Insight, an Idea with Sergey Brin." Filmed January 19, 2017, in Davos-Klosters, Switzerland. World Economic Forum Annual

Meeting video, 34:07. https://www.weforum.org/events/world-economic-forum-annual-meeting-2017.

91. **I wrote an article for *Esquire*:** Galloway, Scott. "Silicon Valley's Tax-Avoiding, Job-Killing, Soul-Sucking Machine." *Esquire*, February 8, 2018.

LOVE

123. **sleeping on their own:** Hollman, Laurie, PhD. "When Should Children Sleep in Their Own Beds?" *Life* (blog), *HuffPost*, November 3,2017. https://www.huffpost.com/entry/when-should-children-slee_b_12662942.

124. **co-sleeping with infants:** "SIDS and Other Sleep-Related Infant Deaths: Expansion of Recommendations for a Safe Infant Sleeping Environment." *Pediatrics* 128, no. 5 (November 2011). http://pediatrics.aappublications.org/content/128/5/1030?sid=ffa523b4-9b5d-492c-a3d1-80de22504e1d.

124. **Japanese are big on co-sleeping:** Murray Buechner, Maryanne. "How to Parent Like the Japanese Do." *Time*, July 17, 2015. http://time.com/3959168/how-to-parent-like-the-japanese-do.

138. **Mark Greene argues:** Greene, Mark. "Touch Isolation: How Homophobia Has Robbed All Men of Touch." Medium, August 7, 2017. https://medium.com/@remakingmanhood/touch-isolation-how-homophobia-has-robbed-all-men-of-touch-239987952f16.

138. **Touch is truly fundamental:** Keltner, Dacher. "Hands On Research: The Science of Touch." *Greater Good*, September 29, 2010. https://greatergood.berkeley.edu/article/item/hands_on_research.

144. **fifty times faster:** Galloway, Scott. "L2 Predictions Instagram Will Be the Most Powerful Social Platform in the World." November 26, 2014. L2inc video, 1:24. https://www.youtube.com/watch?v=9bF9PF0Yvjs&feature=youtu.be&t=43.

144. **images of our early childhood:** Heshmat, Shahram, PhD. "Why Do We Remember Certain Things, But Forget Others?: How the Experience of Emotion Enhances Our Memories." *Psychology Today*, October 2015. https://www.psychologytoday.com/blog/science-choice/201510/why-do-we-remember-certain-things-forget-others.

165. **stepmothers and stepfathers:** Whiting, David. "O.C. Divorce Rate One of Highest in Nation." *Orange County Register*, June 25, 2012. http://www.ocregister.com/2012/06/25/oc-divorce-rate-one-of-highest-in-nation.

168. **a better fucking phone:** Galloway, Scott. "Cash & Denting the Universe." *Daily Insights*, Gartner L2, May 5, 2017. https://www.l2inc.com/daily-insights/no-mercy-no-malice/cash-denting-the-universe.

171. **fast and slow thinking:** Kahneman, Daniel. *Thinking, Fast and Slow.* New York: Farrar, Straus and Giroux, 2011.

178. **homeless dotting the sidewalks:** Editorial. "6,686: A Civic Disgrace." *San Francisco Chronicle,* July 3, 2016. http://projects.sfchronicle.com/sf-homeless/civic-disgrace.

178. **"make the world a better place":** https://qz.com/563375/all-the-philanthropic-causes-near-and-dear-to-the-hearts-of-mark-zuckerberg-and-priscilla-chan.

178. **software and driverless cars:** Hudack, Mike. "San Francisco: Now with More Dystopia." *Mike Hudack* (blog). October 1, 2017. https://www.mhudack.com/blog/2017/10/1/san-francisco-now-with-more-dystopia.

179. **picking the right career:** Galloway, Scott. "Prof Galloway's Career Advice." August 31, 2017. L2inc video, 3:54. https://www.youtube.com/watch?v=1T22QxTkPoM&t=5s.

180. **wider than his seat:** Elliott, Christopher. "Your Airplane Seat Is Going to Keep Shrinking." *Fortune,* September 12, 2015. http://fortune.com/2015/09/12/airline-seats-shrink.

183. **pay another 27 cents:** Petersen, Gene. "Why You Might Not Actually Need Premium Gas." *Consumer Reports,* May 7, 2018. https://www.consumerreports.org/fuel-economy-efficiency/why-you-might-not-actually-need-premium-gas.

185. **85 percent of post-recession:** Close, Kerry. "The 1% Pocketed 85% of Post-Recession Income Growth." *Time,* June 16, 2016. http://time.com/money/4371332/income-inequality-recession.

HEALTH

215. **Being a jerk to an Uber driver:** Newcomer, Eric. "In Video, Uber CEO Argues with Driver Over Falling Fares." *Bloomberg,* February 28, 2017. https://www.bloomberg.com/news /articles/2017-02-28/in-video-uber-ceo-argues-with-driver -over-falling-fares.

216. **Gratitude helps people:** Harvard Health Publishing. "Giving Thanks Can Make You Happier," Healthbeat. https://www .health.harvard.edu/healthbeat/giving-thanks-can-make -you-happier.

218. **Why is a fifty-four-year-old professor:** Galloway, Scott (@prof-galloway). https://twitter.com/profgalloway.

SCOTT GALLOWAY is the *New York Times* bestselling author of *The Four: The Hidden DNA of Amazon, Apple, Facebook, and Google* and a professor at New York University's Stern School of Business. A serial entrepreneur, he has founded nine firms, including L2, Red Envelope, and Prophet. In 2012, he was named one of the "World's 50 Best Business School Professors" by Poets & Quants. His weekly YouTube series, "Winners & Losers," has generated tens of millions of views. He is the co-host of *Pivot* with Recode's Kara Swisher and the author of the newsletter No Mercy / No Malice.

Also by Scott Galloway

PORTFOLIO
PENGUIN

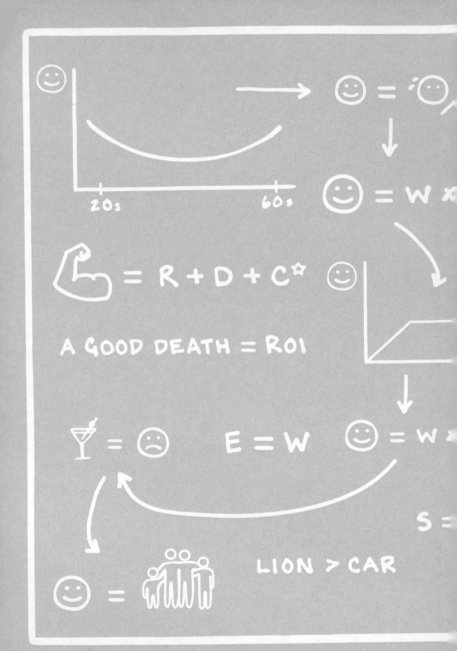